M000189777

# The Meaning of Motherhood

# The Meaning of Motherhood

*Discovering Joy and Purpose Through Christ
in the Everyday Moments of Mom Life*

Alexandra Jensen

RESOURCE *Publications* · Eugene, Oregon

THE MEANING OF MOTHERHOOD
Discovering Joy and Purpose Through Christ in the Everyday
Moments of Mom Life

Copyright © 2022 Alexandra Jensen. All rights reserved. Except for brief quotations in critical publications or reviews, no part of this book may be reproduced in any manner without prior written permission from the publisher. Write: Permissions, Wipf and Stock Publishers, 199 W. 8th Ave., Suite 3, Eugene, OR 97401.

Resource Publications
An Imprint of Wipf and Stock Publishers
199 W. 8th Ave., Suite 3
Eugene, OR 97401

www.wipfandstock.com

PAPERBACK ISBN: 978-1-6667-4770-6
HARDCOVER ISBN: 978-1-6667-4771-3
EBOOK ISBN: 978-1-6667-4772-0

07/29/22

All Scripture quotations, unless otherwise indicated, are taken from the Holy Bible, New International Version®, NIV®. Copyright ©1973, 1978, 1984, 2011 by Biblica, Inc.™ Used by permission of Zondervan. All rights reserved worldwide. www.zondervan.comThe "NIV" and "New International Version" are trademarks registered in the United States Patent and Trademark Office by Biblica, Inc.™

To my wonderful, loving husband. You are my best friend. Thank you for supporting me in all of my endeavors, and being the rock of our family.

# Contents

# Chapter 1

# The Meaning

As a stay at home mom, I used to wonder if my life really mattered. I would wake up each morning, as a sense of purposelessness washed over me. That was until I washed my face, opened up my Bible and heard what the Lord had to say! The truth is, I don't have to make a dent in the whole world, I just need to make a dent in the little worlds God has placed right in front of me. My 2½ year old daughter, Emma Claire, my 13 month old son, Josiah, and my husband *need me!* They need my presence. They love me, and God does too.

Maybe you can relate? You may be a new mom or a more experienced mother than I am, still struggling with the same old story. *What is my purpose?* You may wonder.

Motherhood is filled with purpose. God often used those hidden from society in miraculous ways. Think about the life of Noah, David, Hannah, and Mary. Noah built the ark by himself for years and years before the floodwaters rose. David spent his days in isolation watching sheep before being appointed King of Israel. Hannah was barren for many years, feeling alone in her struggles, before bearing God's chosen prophet and judge of Israel, Samuel.

Mary was a young woman, of low prestige in Biblical times, who bore the Savior of the World.

Being a mom matters! It matters more than you and I will ever know on this side of Heaven. Jesus wants to use us in some pretty big ways. He is shaping us to be strong moms, able to help form our little men and women's hearts to reflect God's image and plan for their lives.

This is not a task for the light of heart and we need to take heart, knowing that God is using us on a daily basis, for His Kingdom purposes, in our homes. On the days when you struggle with the lie that your life lacks meaning, put on your "Mama" hat and remember that according to Jesus your life matters! In the midst of changing diapers, reading stories before naptime, preparing lunches, snacks, and sippy cups, know that God is watching you. He is watching over you and working through you. Your every little interaction with your child is noted by your Lord and Savior, Jesus Christ. Make it count!

Buckle in and strap up, because being a mom of littles is a wild ride, and something tells me the roller coaster does not stop at age 5. Being a mom is for a lifetime. Praise the Lord! Your children are always going to need you. "Once a mom, always a mom." I have heard it said. I know this to be true, because there are times when I still need my own mom and mother in law in big ways.

I am incredibly thankful for the women in my life who have shaped me, and it is encouraging to know that it is my turn now. The torch has been passed and it is my time to raise my children with all my might, bringing them up in the Fear and Love of the Lord, teaching them right from wrong, correcting, discipling, and teaching them about Jesus. Teaching them about Jesus through God's Word and by example is my job. However, I know that I am not alone, and that others want to come along beside me and help my children along the way. "It takes a village to raise a child." This is true! I pray that I would help surround my children with godly influences, friends and adults with this same godly mission in mind: to raise up disciples who love Jesus and spread God's love to others. This is the overarching meaning and purpose of motherhood; to raise men and women who love the Lord God with all their hearts and love their neighbors as themselves (Matthew 22:37-39).

*"Teacher, which is the greatest commandment in the Law?"*

*Jesus replied: "'Love the Lord your God with all your heart and with all your soul and with all your mind.' This is the first and greatest commandment. And the second is like it: 'Love your neighbor as yourself.' Matthew 22:36-39 (NIV)*

The second greatest commandment, "Love your neighbor as yourself," speaks to me as a mom. Who are my neighbors? -Those next to me. Each day, my children do life beside me and therefore, they are my neighbors. Considering my children in this light, I must love them as I love myself. I feed myself, I take care of my body, and I nourish my soul each day with God's Word and through prayer. I must love my children in this same way.

Although my children are young, I can still pray with them before they go to bed and before naptime. Although they are young, I can read small portions of God's Word to them from their Children's Bible. Although they are young, I can still sing songs about Jesus to them. Although they are young, I can still set an example of godliness for them. Society is trying to take Jesus out of the equation, therefore we need to work and be intentional about incorporating Jesus into our lives, with our children, each day.

The abbreviation "BC" stands for "before Christ." The abbreviation "AD" stands for *annō Dominī*, which translates to "in the year of the Lord." However, history books are now changing and referring to what was commonly known as BC to BCE, which stands for "before common era." AD is being changed to CE, "common era." In making this switch, the world is taking Christ out of the equation. Although the time periods are the same, without reference to Christ, young hearts and minds may never know the true meaning of this time period referral. It has everything to do with Jesus, and while some may argue that the time period is the same and maintains the same connotation in reference to Christ, they are doing away with his holy name. That is a major problem! By not naming Christ, we invalidate the truth and power of all that he did for us on the cross. We must remember Jesus. We must proclaim his holy name.

At home, at school, out and about, at the grocery store, driving in the car, we must tune in our children's hearts and minds to hear the name of Jesus. We must speak of him and help our children remain in touch with the significance of his name. The world is not going to do it for us. As moms, we must take the initiative to immerse our children's thoughts in Christ.

I've heard it said, "Be the kind of woman you want your daughter to be." Another way that it has been explained is, "Be the kind of wife you would want your son to marry." Having a son of my own puts this quote in the light of a magnified perspective. I do want my son to marry a godly, faith filled woman. I do want my son to live happily ever after someday with a submissive, respectful wife. I do want my son's bride to be full of God's love. Therefore, I must cultivate these attributes within myself and set an example of a godly woman.

Proverbs 31 describes a wife, or woman of noble character:

*A wife of noble character who can find?*
*She is worth far more than rubies.*
*Her husband has full confidence in her*
*and lacks nothing of value.*
*She brings him good, not harm,*
*all the days of her life.*
*She selects wool and flax*
*and works with eager hands.*
*She is like the merchant ships,*
*bringing her food from afar.*
*She gets up while it is still night;*
*she provides food for her family*
*and portions for her female servants.*
*She considers a field and buys it;*
*out of her earnings she plants a vineyard.*
*She sets about her work vigorously;*
*her arms are strong for her tasks.*

*She sees that her trading is profitable,*
>*and her lamp does not go out at night.*
*In her hand she holds the distaff*
>*and grasps the spindle with her fingers.*
*She opens her arms to the poor*
>*and extends her hands to the needy.*
*When it snows, she has no fear for her household;*
>*for all of them are clothed in scarlet.*
*She makes coverings for her bed;*
>*she is clothed in fine linen and purple.*
*Her husband is respected at the city gate,*
>*where he takes his seat among the elders of the land.*
*She makes linen garments and sells them,*
>*and supplies the merchants with sashes.*
*She is clothed with strength and dignity;*
>*she can laugh at the days to come.*
*She speaks with wisdom,*
>*and faithful instruction is on her tongue.*
*She watches over the affairs of her household*
>*and does not eat the bread of idleness.*
*Her children arise and call her blessed;*
>*her husband also, and he praises her:*
*"Many women do noble things,*
>*but you surpass them all."*
*Charm is deceptive, and beauty is fleeting;*
>*but a woman who fears the Lord is to be praised.*
*(Proverbs 31:10-30)*

What does being a Proverbs 31 woman look like in today's world? Being a woman of The Word is the very first trait that comes to mind. Being a woman who is in God's Word daily is so so important when it comes to being a God filled, Christ loving creation as a mom and wife. God's Word really is living, breathing, and active, sharper than a double edged sword. It will cut straight to the heart and reveal yuckiness that you never even knew was there. God's

Word will refine you, but you have to adopt reading God's Word as a daily discipline and read it with the purpose of knowing and loving God. Rather than self gratification, let God's Word edify you by learning about God's character and the nature of Christ.

> For the word of God is alive and active. Sharper than any double-edged sword, it penetrates even to divide soul and spirit, joints and marrow; it judges the thoughts and attitudes of the heart. (Hebrew 4:12)

While I do want you to continue reading and enjoying this book, I want you to get into God's Word. Make it a point to put God's Word first when it comes to your daily reading. Christian Living and self help books are great. I am a huge fan, but I am also guilty of neglecting time spent in God's Word because I was too caught up in reading a particular Christian self help book. In order to get the most out of this book, you need to be reading God's Word first and foremost. It will change your life, and daily perspective.

## Let Me Come Alongside You!

My goal is to encourage you in your faith as a mom and a wife. I am not perfect and will be the first one to admit that I have many faults. I am going to be as transparent as possible throughout the course of this book, in order to help you better relate, and realize that you are not alone.

When I first became a mom, I had this magical idea of what motherhood would be like. When we brought our baby girl, Emma Claire, home from the hospital, reality set in. Sleepless nights, makeupless days spent in my pajamas, lethargy, and the baby blues all set into effect. I was a wreck. I needed my Lord and Savior to step in and declare meaning and purpose over my life. I needed Jesus to show me how to have a schedule in being a brand new (stay at home) mom. I needed God to breathe his life giving presence into my new lifestyle. I needed scripture to meditate on. I needed other Mama friends. I was lost as a new mom, and in desperate need of Jesus' love, support, friendship, and stamp of approval.

I soon learned after becoming a mom that motherhood is no cake walk. It is not only physically challenging, but also mentally taxing. The constant crying, the midnight feedings, having little to no adult interaction throughout the day, the fluctuating hormones, *Mama I know what it is like.* I have walked in your shoes. I can't take the torch from your weary arm or offer you anything other than Jesus' strength, love, and comfort, but let me come alongside you as a friend who has been there. Let me speak life into your weary soul through what Jesus says, according to God's Word.

> *"Come to me, all you who are weary and burdened, and I will give you rest. Take my yoke upon you and learn from me, for I am gentle and humble in heart, and you will find rest for your souls. For my yoke is easy and my burden is light." Matthew 11:28-30*

I can't take the torch from you, but I know a man who can. His name is Jesus. The more we depend on him for love, friendship, and daily support, the stronger our faith becomes. Let the monumental presence of Jesus in your life overcome your daily struggles. Let the wisdom, love, and power of Christ fill your heart.

You are not alone in your struggles. You are not alone in your feelings of inadequacy or purposelessness. You are not alone in your sadness and what can feel like the sacrifice of your dreams and life plans. You are not alone in motherhood. God is with you. He wants to meet you right where you are at in the ordinary and mundane moments of washing dishes, changing diapers, driving to dance lessons, brushing baby teeth, bottle feeding, bath and bedtime. You are not alone. God is with you, and I feel for you! We are in the same boat mama. I am praying for you. I love you as a sister in Christ although we may never meet on this side of heaven.

Can I pray for you?

*Dear Jesus,*

*We know you and we love you. Thank you for your daily presence in our lives. Please strengthen our hearts as we go about each day feeding, loving, and taking care of our children. Come alongside us Jesus, and be our strength.*

*On days that feel dry and our hearts are thirsty for some-
thing more, I pray that we will draw from the well of your
source of truth in our daily lives, God's Word. Help us
to uncover your guiding light through the Bible. Thank
you for your Word, and for loving us fiercely. We love you
Lord Jesus. Amen*

## Steps of Faith:

"Steps of Faith" are practical applications of the chapter's message,
found at the end of each chapter. How can you live out what you've
just read, and take a step of faith toward the cross? Some steps will
seem like baby strides while other days will feel like giant leaps! Let
us live out our calling as Moms in Christ and walk by faith.

*For we walk by faith, not by sight. Yes, we are of good cour-
age, and we would rather be away from the body and at
home with the Lord. So whether we are at home or away, we
make it our aim to please him. 2 Corinthians 5:7-9 (ESV)*

## Steps of Faith:

- Read back through Proverbs 31 and pray that the Lord would
  mold you into the image of a mother and wife after God's
  own heart.

## Chapter 2

# Come to the Well

*When a Samaritan woman came to draw water, Jesus said to her, "Will you give me a drink?" (His disciples had gone into the town to buy food.)*

*The Samaritan woman said to him, "You are a Jew and I am a Samaritan woman. How can you ask me for a drink?" (For Jews do not associate with Samaritans.)*

*Jesus answered her, "If you knew the gift of God and who it is that asks you for a drink, you would have asked him and he would have given you living water."*

*"Sir," the woman said, "you have nothing to draw with and the well is deep. Where can you get this living water? Are you greater than our father Jacob, who gave us the well and drank from it himself, as did also his sons and his livestock?"*

*Jesus answered, "Everyone who drinks this water will be thirsty again, but whoever drinks the water I give them will never thirst. Indeed, the water I give them will become in them a spring of water welling up to eternal life."*
*(John 4:7-14)*

Have you ever been thirsty? I mean, like really thirsty? One time, I was hiking with my husband in the beautiful countryside of Arkansas, and we had to physically carry our own supply of water on our backs. Being an avid water drinker, I tried rationing my water supply as best as I could but quickly into our adventure, my water supply ran out. I was thirsty. Toward the end of the day, I was really thirsty, and my loving, kind husband shared some of his water with me. This episode made me think of the woman at the well in the Bible. She shared her water with Jesus and received eternal life in return. She was desperate and craved something that no physical water could ever satisfy. Can you relate?

Sometimes as a mom I get stuck in a "grass is greener on the other side" mentality. If I could just go back to work, then I would be happy. If I could just go on a girl's trip. If I could only get a babysitter more often. I have run into a lot of "If I could onlys" in my lifetime. The truth is, we need to learn how to be content right where we are at. In this very season, God is teaching and remaking me. He is transforming me from the inside out through motherhood and I know that He is preparing me for seasons to come. Still, I know that some days are hard and being truly content is easier said than done. I want to encourage you and let you know that what you are feeling is normal, but we must fight to maintain the mindset of Christ. We must strive for holiness, peace, and joy. Being thankful is a great tool that we can use to fight our feelings of "life is not fair," "this mom gig is too tough," "I need more 'me time,'" and so many more perilous thoughts that threaten our contentment.

Make a numbered list of things you are grateful for. In this way, we can literally count our blessings and realize all that we do have instead of dwelling on that which we do not. Try to think of at least 10 things you are grateful for in your life today.

Count Your Blessings:

1.

2.

3.

4.

5.

6.

7.

8.

9.

10.

Having a spirit of thanksgiving overflows into every single area of our lives, including motherhood. Learning how to be joyful in seasons that are difficult is easier done when thankfulness is present. Before you start dwelling on the greener grass on the other side of motherhood, be thankful for the day and the little blessings along the way.

We must draw from the well of Christ's Living Water, available to us through the Holy Spirit in order to find our fulfillment in Christ. We have the presence of Jesus alive in us, and this changes everything. We have the power to draw from the well, our source of peace and life through Christ, because of his presence.

## A Gentle Whisper

I am a mom of two littles, and some days are extremely tough, both physically and emotionally. These are the days when I need Christ the most. On days when I feel at my weakest, I must rely on Christ's strength.

> *Three times I pleaded with the Lord to take it away from me. But he said to me, "My grace is sufficient for you, for my power is made perfect in weakness." Therefore I will boast all the more gladly about my weaknesses, so that Christ's power may rest on me. That is why, for Christ's*

*sake, I delight in weaknesses, in insults, in hardships, in persecutions, in difficulties. For when I am weak, then I am strong.* 2 Corinthians 12:8-10

Today, reading my Bible, the precursory verse to 2 Corinthians 12:9 stuck out to me, verse 8, which states, "three times I pleaded with the Lord to take it away from me." Yet the Lord did not take it from him. The thorn in Paul's flesh remained present, but God did provide him with an answer to his prayer that made him lean in on Christ like never before.

Have you ever pleaded with the Lord for something; a new job, a baby, a spouse, or some sort of change in your life? I know I certainly have. Sometimes the Lord delivers us from whatever is plaguing us. Sometimes the answer to a prayer is a sudden yes, but other times the answer may be a resounding no. Other times the answer may be yet to come, and we are invited to sit at Jesus' feet and wait. Many times, the answer shows up in the exact opposite form than what we expected.

In the book of 1 Kings, the story of Elijah, the prophet Elijah flees for his life after God's divine encounter on Mount Carmel. Elijah had just killed all of the false prophets of Baal during the time of King Ahab and Queen Jezebel's reign. Jezebel sought vengeance for the prophets Elijah slayed. Elijah fled for his life, and the Lord appeared to him.

*And the word of the Lord came to him: "What are you doing here, Elijah?"*

*He replied, "I have been very zealous for the Lord God Almighty. The Israelites have rejected your covenant, torn down your altars, and put your prophets to death with the sword. I am the only one left, and now they are trying to kill me too."*

*The Lord said, "Go out and stand on the mountain in the presence of the Lord, for the Lord is about to pass by."*

*Then a great and powerful wind tore the mountains apart and shattered the rocks before the Lord, but the Lord was not in the wind. After the wind there was an earthquake,*

*but the Lord was not in the earthquake. After the earth-
quake came a fire, but the Lord was not in the fire. And
after the fire came a gentle whisper. (1 Kings 19:9-12)*

The Lord was not in the wind, earthquake, or fire; but rather in
a gentle whisper. God does not always answer our prayers or show
up in the ways we expect. Oftentimes it is more subtle, ordinary,
or simply different than our expectations. Let us not limit God
by placing extraordinary expectations on his encounters with us.
Rather, let us look for God in the quiet, in the still, in the mundane,
and even the dull moments of motherhood. When all of our hope
is dried out and we cry out to Jesus, let us not lose faith, because
sometimes his response to our heart desires may look or sound
a little different than what we had prayed for, or were expecting.
Sometimes the Lord truly does show up in a gentle whisper rather
than the fire, wind, or earthquake answer we were anticipating, and
maybe even hoping for. The truth is, his plans for us are good, always. They may not feel good at times, but they are always for the
best in our lives to unfold. His plans are to prosper and not to harm
us, to give us hope and a future (Jeremiah 29:11). Based on the past,
based on the scriptures, God's pattern of faithfulness never fails. He
will never leave, forsake, or fail you (Hebrews 13:5).

## Do It

One day, I was feeling especially discouraged after being at home
all day by myself taking care of my 8 month and 2 year old. It was
not until bedtime that I heard the quiet whisper I had been praying for so desperately hours before. My little two year old said two
words that shifted something inside of me that night at bedtime.
After jammies were put on, teeth were brushed, and books were
read, she said "Mommy pray." I was about to leave the room and
this startled and flooded my heart with excitement. I had forgotten
to pray with her and she was subtly reminding me in her two year
old way, "Mommy pray." We certainly did pray, and as I left her
bedroom telling her all sorts of sweet goodnights, "night night,"

"sweet dreams," "I love you," "sleep tight," "see you in the morning," and "goodnight" my heart was filled with joy and my mindset was overwhelmed with a fresh sense of purpose and love for my role as that precious little girl's mother.

Emma Claire needs me, but even more so she needs Jesus. And she needs me to provide an arrow that points to Jesus, every single day. Even at such an early age, we make a huge difference in our children's lives. Our role as Christ followers is to "Go and make disciples of all nations, baptizing them in the name of the Father and of the Son and of the Holy Spirit" (Matthew 28:19). But what if "go" really means "do it." Wherever you are at, in your home, at work, wherever God has placed you, whoever he has placed you around, make disciples. *Do it.*

In Matthew 19:14 Jesus said, "Let the little children come to me, and do not hinder them, for the kingdom of heaven belongs to such as these." What does it mean to hinder? In the verse prior to Matthew 19:14, verse 13 says "Then people brought little children to Jesus for him to place his hands on them and pray for them. But the disciples rebuked them." "Rebuke" is a synonym for "hinder," but "stop" "hamper" and "impede" are also synonyms. The dictionary definition of hinder is, "to prevent from doing, acting, or happening."

Are we providing our children with ample opportunities to see and hear from Jesus? We need to be praying with our children, speaking scripture over them, and verbally acknowledging Jesus each day. In this way, we can let our children come to Jesus, and not hinder them. Notice the word "little," in verse 19:14. Exposing our children to Christ should start at an early age.

"For the Kingdom of Heaven belongs to such as these." As adults, we need to adopt a childlike faith and fully rely on the Lord once again. In the same way that we were once on fire for God as new believers, we need to get back to that.

*Truly I tell you, anyone who will not receive the kingdom of God like a little child will never enter it. Luke 18:17*

Having a faith that is simple, pure, and wholly trusts in the Lord like a naive child is such a precious thing in the Lord's sight. Furthermore, humility is of the essence when it comes to having a childlike faith. In Biblical times, you were low in status as a child. Jesus seemed to favor those of low status and provided extra love and support to the poor, widows, the sick, and those with disabilities. In the same way, we must humble ourselves and come to him realizing our desperate need and desire for Jesus, each day.

> *For we do not have a high priest who is unable to empathize with our weaknesses, but we have one who has been tempted in every way, just as we are—yet he did not sin. Let us then approach God's throne of grace with confidence, so that we may receive mercy and find grace to help us in our time of need. Hebrews 4:15-16*

I can vividly imagine a child approaching God's throne of grace with a sense of bold confidence and a certain level of naiveness. Children are very impressionable at an early age. That is why it is so important that we immerse them in the Gospel when they are young. We do this through placing them in Sunday school, going to church weekly, and by listening to Christian music. We do this through conversation revolving around Christ, singing "Jesus Loves Me This I Know . . . " and so many other ways. But it does not come naturally. We have to be intentional.

Be sure you are drawing from the well each day, God's source of truth and life, the Bible. You will be better equipped to lead your children when you are being led and fed by your Savior and Shepherd each day. Make it a point to pray. I have to set a five minute timer on my apple watch and physically get down on my hands and knees each day. Maybe prayer time looks a little different for you. That is okay. It is also important to pray throughout the day, but having a few moments of uninterrupted prayer time is powerful. It will change you. It will change your perspective of God and draw you close to his heart.

Quench your heart's thirst by relying on the Lord God, and the Bible to sustain you. As moms, it is easy to get caught up in constantly looking around for external things to fill us. *I am guilty!* Until we stop looking around for shiny things and start looking up to the sky, seeking the source of where our help comes from, we will continue to feel empty inside.

Christ wants to share his water supply with you. He can cause his holy water to trickle and even gush down from Heaven in order to heal, fill, and help you grow. You need only to have faith in the rain.

> He replied, "Because you have so little faith. Truly I tell you, if you have faith as small as a mustard seed, you can say to this mountain, 'Move from here to there,' and it will move. Nothing will be impossible for you." *Matthew 17:20*

Meditate on this Psalm as a prayer:

> Lord, you alone are my portion and my cup;
>     you make my lot secure.
> The boundary lines have fallen for me in pleasant places;
>     surely I have a delightful inheritance.
> I will praise the Lord, who counsels me;
>     even at night my heart instructs me.
> I keep my eyes always on the Lord.
>     With him at my right hand, I will not be shaken.
> Therefore my heart is glad and my tongue rejoices;
>     my body also will rest secure,
> because you will not abandon me to the realm of the dead,
>     nor will you let your faithful one see decay.
> You make known to me the path of life;
>     you will fill me with joy in your presence,
>     with eternal pleasures at your right hand.
> Psalm 16:5-11

Steps of Faith:

- Get into God's Word today! Try reading a Psalm, Proverb, and one chapter of a New Testament book of your choice from the Bible.

- In what way can you "do it?" What daily patterns can you implement to help your kids be immersed in the knowledge and love of Christ? Prayer before bedtime, prayer before naps, reading a children's Bible with your kids, purchasing and listening to a children's praise and worship album or CD in the car. Apply one new activity, and practice it daily. Do it!

Chapter 3

# Look Up!

I have introverted tendencies. Creative, gifted, introverted extrovert; whichever way you would like to spin the record. I almost used the word special, but then I find myself digging through the trashcan to find something I accidentally threw away, and picking up broken chips off the kitchen floor that my toddler tossed from her high chair like pennies into a dried up wishing well. I notice a spider crawling up the wall and attempt to smash it, but I knock over and shatter an empty Topo Chico bottle instead. I begin to sweep up the shards using a damp paper towel because my broom is still "MIA" from our most recent move. My finger starts bleeding, the baby is crying, and the laundry dryer alarm is going off as if the cavalry is coming, although it is really not, and I desperately wish it was. *Does anyone else share these same long sufferings?*

I wondered these things to myself as I continued to scavenge the kitchen floor and found a few blueberries. Quickly, I popped them into my mouth, as to prove myself unabashed, only to find shame and loneliness had already crept in like "Shoe Goo" being opened after a high altitude flight. I stayed down. I sat on my filthy kitchen floor, and for a hot minute, it almost felt like the enemy had won. Past the point of tears, I simply sat, pondering my life and questioning my very existence.

Through the emotional mess, God's voice found me, *I love you Alexandra, as I love all my children. I do not love them equally as if my love were a linear scale. I love you individually. I love you separately. I love you for the unique, daring, strong, bold and beautiful young lady you can be, but only through Me.*

The Lauren Daigle song "Look Up Child" chimed in on the background, and I realized it was no small coincidence. Not only did I need to "look up," I needed to get up! I needed to adopt a positive attitude. I needed to select words of cheer as if they were lifesaving medicine. I needed to pop open my Bible like a bottle of champagne to celebrate my newfound victory in Christ.

*I can do this.* I told myself. *I can be an amazing wife, mother, and homemaker. I can cook! I can sell antiques and hire a maid to help me clean. I am going to figure this thing out! I am going to rock this crazy, beautiful, messy life God has given me. In Jesus, for Jesus, and through Jesus. Help me Lord, Amen.* With that, I shot up off the kitchen floor with rocket fuel propulsion.

> *Why am I discouraged?*
> *Why is my heart so sad?*
> *I will put my hope in God!*
> *I will praise him again*
> *My Savior and my God!*
> *Psalm 42:11 (NLT)*

Do you ever have moments like this in motherhood? Moments that make you wonder if what you are doing really matters. I used to have them more often than not, until I stopped feeling sorry for myself, and realized that what I do really and truly does matter. It matters to my kids and my husband, but most of all it matters to the Lord.

> "Whoever can be trusted with very little can also be trusted with much, and whoever is dishonest with very little will also be dishonest with much." *Luke 16:10*

This verse has been on my heart and mind a lot lately. We are called to be faithful. As moms and wives, our faithfulness is important to the heart of God. In endeavors big and small, consider your faithfulness to the task and perform your daily duties with the mindset that God is watching. He most certainly is, and he most certainly cares that you give this thing called life, and motherhood your all!

The Lord is my strength and portion each day. Some days are more difficult than others, but I have found that as long as I am getting in the Word, and getting on my hands and knees to pray, it is going to be an okay day! I encourage you to get into God's Word and pray today.

*I lift up my eyes to the mountains—*
*where does my help come from?*
*My help comes from the Lord,*
*the Maker of heaven and earth.*
Psalm 121:1-2

## Three Essential Ingredients of Prayer

Prayer does not have to be a monumental, daunting task. However, there are some bullet points to prayer that can help you better communicate with the Lord. Three components of prayer that have helped me are: Praise, Forgiveness, and Petition (P.F.P.).

Praise- Praise is simply going before the Lord and acknowledging his blessings in your life. Thanking God for all he has done and for all that is yet to come is a crucial part of prayer. Praise him for his faithful character. Praise him for his Word. Praise him through Psalms. Praise him by pouring out your heart of gratitude for his blessings.

Forgiveness- Ask the Lord to forgive you of your sins daily. Ask him to reveal any pieces or parts of you that are not holy and pleasing to God. Repent and turn from your sin.

Petition- Petition is asking the Lord for certain things to unfold in your life. For example, I pray every day that my children will come to know, love, and live for Christ. This is a form of petition.

Praise, Forgiveness, Petition (P.F.P.)—Praying in this order puts my prayer requests into perspective and helps me to clear my heart and mind before the petition process.

## Bible Study Journaling Questions

When I get into God's Word, I often rely on three basic questions that help lead me through the scripture passage. The following questions lead me through studying God's Word by journaling.

- What is the main point of the passage?
- What does this teach you about the nature of God?
- Does this passage connect with or remind you of any other verses?

If time allows, include this additional, bonus question in your journaling quiet time:

- How can you apply this knowledge of scripture to your life?

## Let's Practice!

*Hebrews 10:1-18:*

*The law is only a shadow of the good things that are coming—not the realities themselves. For this reason it can never, by the same sacrifices repeated endlessly year after year, make perfect those who draw near to worship. Otherwise, would they not have stopped being offered? For the worshipers would have been cleansed once for all, and would no longer have felt guilty for their sins. But those sacrifices are an annual reminder of sins. It is impossible for the blood of bulls and goats to take away sins.*

*Therefore, when Christ came into the world, he said:*

*"Sacrifice and offering you did not desire,*
*but a body you prepared for me;*
*with burnt offerings and sin offerings*
*you were not pleased.*
*Then I said, 'Here I am—it is written about me*
*in the scroll—*
*I have come to do your will, my God.'"*

*First he said, "Sacrifices and offerings, burnt offerings and*
*sin offerings you did not desire, nor were you pleased with*
*them"—though they were offered in accordance with the*
*law. Then he said, "Here I am, I have come to do your will."*
*He sets aside the first to establish the second. And by that*
*will, we have been made holy through the sacrifice of the*
*body of Jesus Christ once for all.*

*Day after day every priest stands and performs his reli-*
*gious duties; again and again he offers the same sacrifices,*
*which can never take away sins. But when this priest had*
*offered for all time one sacrifice for sins, he sat down at*
*the right hand of God, and since that time he waits for his*
*enemies to be made his footstool. For by one sacrifice he*
*has made perfect forever those who are being made holy.*

*The Holy Spirit also testifies to us about this. First he says:*

*"This is the covenant I will make with them*
*after that time, says the Lord.*
*I will put my laws in their hearts,*
*and I will write them on their minds."*

*Then he adds:*

*"Their sins and lawless acts*
*I will remember no more."*

*And where these have been forgiven, sacrifice for sin is no*
*longer necessary.*

- What is the main point of the passage?

  The main point of the passage is that Jesus came and was the
  ultimate sacrifice, therefore the sacrifice of animals for our

sins is no longer necessary. We have been made holy through the sacrifice of Jesus, once and for all.

- What does this teach us about the nature of God?

God loves us so much that he sent his only son to save us, and to provide a way for our sins to be atoned for, so that we might experience perfect communion with him forever in Heaven. Through the blood of Christ, through Salvation we are forgiven and set free from the bondage of sin and eternal separation. God is love. God wants to be with us.

- Does this passage connect with or remind you of any other verses?

John 3:16 "For God so loved the world that whoever believes in him shall not perish but have everlasting life."

1 John 4:16 "And so we know and rely on the love God has for us. God is love. Whoever lives in love lives in God, and God in them."

Ephesians 2:8-9 "For it is by grace you have been saved, through faith—and this is not from yourselves, it is the gift of God—not by works, so that no one can boast."

- How can I apply this knowledge of scripture to my life?

I can apply this to my life through my daily living, by offering my life as a sacrifice to Christ through living for him and dying to myself and my sinful nature; striving to live a holy life that is a fragrant offering, pleasing to the Lord God. I can enter the presence of the Lord each day by reading God's Word, praying, and simply communicating with him throughout the day. By acknowledging Christ in all that I do, the Fear of the Lord will consume my thoughts, and the peace of Christ's presence will be with me.

I hope these questions will help you as you study God's Word with the purpose to learn about and glean wisdom from the character and nature of God. If you are looking for a good starting point in your Bible, Romans is a great place to begin. It is a book written by Paul the Apostle that beautifully illustrates the Gospel.

I want you to get to know God. I want you to get to know God not because I told you to, or because you feel like it is what you are supposed to do, but because you love the Lord and want more of his presence in your daily life. Reading the Bible is not meant to be difficult. Do not overcomplicate getting into the Word. Reading God's Word has brought me so much joy and peace in my life, and I wish the same for you Mama!

## An Invitation

If you are not sure what Christ's presence feels like, if you do not know Jesus as your personal Lord and Savior, I want to extend an invitation for you to accept Christ into your heart, to be the King of your life. If you already know Jesus, recommit yourself through prayer.

Pray This Prayer Out Loud:

*Dear Jesus,*

*Today I choose to live for you.*

*Forgive me of my past sins and mistakes. Make me new. Come into my heart. Enter into every area of my life, and be my King.*

*Jesus, you are the Son of the living God. You died on a wooden cross and rose from the grave to save me from sin and eternal darkness. It is the cry of my heart to be with you in Heaven someday. I praise you for the cross, your resurrection, and the free gift of Salvation. I accept you today Jesus. Be the King of my life. Forgive me of my sins. I can't wait to glorify you forever in eternity! Thank you Jesus for saving me. Amen.*

*If you declare with your mouth, "Jesus is Lord," and believe in your heart that God raised him from the dead, you will be saved. For it is with your heart that you believe and are justified, and it is with your mouth that you profess your faith and are saved. Romans 10:9-10 (NIV)*

Below is a list of verses, which speak truth and shine bright light onto who we are not only as mothers, but also as daughters of Christ. These verses uplift me each day, as I refer back to them in my Bible. I highly recommend you do the same!

## Who Am I In Christ?

I am . . .

- Chosen. (Romans 8:31-33)
- Infinitely Loved. (Romans 8:35-39)
- Victorious. (Isaiah 12:2)
- His Prized Possession. (James 1:18)
- Shielded in Christ's Love. (Prov. 3:5)
- An Heir of the Kingdom of God. (Psalm 17:14)
- Claimed. (John 14:18)
- God's Very Own Possession; Capable of Goodness. (1 Peter 2:9)
- A Child of God. (John 1:12)
- Free. (John 15:15)
- Made New. (Romans 5:1)

## Steps of Faith:

- In what small way can you evangelize today? If nothing specific comes to mind, type out and post one of the verses listed above to one of your social media accounts.

## Chapter 4

# Chaos and Order

As mothers we have the special privilege of bringing order to chaos in our homes. In so many different ways this is accomplished. We pick up armies of toys, fold mountains of laundry, brush our children's plaque riddled teeth, wipe the crumbs and mysterious stickiness off our kitchen countertops, and attempt to conquer the never ending cycle of washing dishes. We also help our little children sort through their oversized feelings and emotions each day, and this is no small task!

Call me crazy, but we went to Walt Disney World when my kids were 10 months and 2 years old. We decided that we would bring a replica of Emma Claire's lovey, her beloved "Hoppy." Hoppy is a tattered little bunny who often smells of swiss cheese. Emma Claire has to have Hoppy with her at naptime and bedtime. My husband found an identical Hoppy on Etsy that we decided we should bring with us on the trip so that we didn't lose the real deal. She would never know the difference . . . we were wrong. She knew immediately this was an imposter rabbit! She would not go down at naptime without a fight. She would not go to sleep in the hotel crib. She slept with her daddy those few nights we spent at Disney World. The incognito "Hoppy" simply would not do.

Toddlers have some crazy big emotions for being such little creatures. Toddlers wear their oversized hearts on their sleeves, like a sugar ant toting a giant leaf. I have a confession to make in this regard. I used to be the kind of person who would look down upon other moms whose toddlers were misbehaving or throwing temper tantrums in public. I could not help but mentally judge these moms. Now I know how difficult it can be, and have a great deal of sympathy for other moms whose children are acting out. Toddlers are crazy passionate about what we consider the silliest little things, and it is up to us to reason with them. It is our role to remind them that what they want, or think that they have to have in the moment, may not be what they really need, or what is best for them. Like taking a banana away from a chimpanzee, this can be incredibly difficult at times.

I remember going to the aquarium recently and Emma Claire kept muttering a word that was hard to decipher initially. It sounded like "yo yo pop." What she was saying was, "lollipop." *Why does she keep saying lollipop?* I wondered. That's when it hit me! The last time we were at the aquarium, my parents, Emma Claire's grandparents, "Mamie" and "Bear" were with us and Bear bought her a lollipop from the giftshop. She remembered. She threw a huge temper tantrum on the way out of the aquarium, insisting upon having a lollipop. If there's anything I have learned about toddler temper tantrums, it is this, *do not feed the beast.* If you give in to their whines and cries and get them what they want, they know their tactics work and are bound to have more temper tantrums in the future. All of this being said, Emma Claire did not get a lollipop that day. She wanted one, but did not need one. In this same way, our Heavenly Father knows what is best for us as his children.

## Order Brought to Chaos in the Scriptures

God consistently brings order to chaos in the scriptures. Sin causes chaos and conflict among people, but God faithfully brings order to our lives, undeserved. In the Old Testament, when The Tower of Babel was formed in the plains of Shinar, God punished the people by dividing their languages, causing a separation of nations. These nations were often at war with each other, and against God's people of Israel. But, the Lord provided order in Israel through different judges like Gideon, Samson, and Jephthah who enabled temporary peace. The Lord established order through the kingdom of Saul and David. David could not construct the temple because he had "blood on his hands" from a lifetime of off and on war. Solomon, a man of peace, constructed the temple, which established order in Israel, but Solomon's reign ended in division due to sin and conflict within his own household, thus establishing the Northern and Southern tribes of Israel and Judah.

The genealogy of Christ is interesting in that there are many unexpected characters that come before Christ. In this royal bloodline are a few women with murky pasts. Tamar, the daughter in law of Judah, the son of Isaac and Leah, married both of Judah's sons on separate accounts, both of whom died early because they disobeyed the Lord. Judah would not marry Tamar to another one of his sons, which was customary, because he feared losing yet again another son. Tamar tricked Judah into thinking she was a prostitute one evening, conceived, and gave birth to Perez who is in the lineage of Christ.

Rahab was a prostitute, known for sheltering two Hebrew spies within the walls of Jericho. It is unknown whether or not Salmon was one of those spies, although it is predicted. Salmon married Rahab after the fall of Jericho and the lineage of Christ continued through Boaz.

Bathsheba was another man's wife when King David lusted after her and unlawfully committed adultery with her. King David intentionally placed Bathsheba's husband, Uriah, on the front lines of battle where he was killed. Bathsheba's first baby with King David was killed on account of their sin, but they had another son, Solomon who would continue Christ's lineage.

It seems a little chaotic that the Lord would weave dark storylines within the backgrounds of Christ's ancestors. However, the Lord was able to create something lovely, a story of redemption evident through this patterned woven blanket. The dark places create eye catching, unique contrasts that add to the grace of this grand masterpiece. Although there are dark places woven throughout, the tapestry of Christ's genealogy is beautiful and full of grace.

There is a pattern in the Bible, where God uses unexpected people to carry out his divine missions. The Lord can use us despite our pasts for his purposes. Just like he was able to use Tamar, Rahab, and Bathsheba who clearly made mistakes, he is able to use us for his plans. We are called to receive his mercy and boldly approach Christ's throne with confidence (Hebrews 4:16). The Lord can forgive us our sins and use us in powerful ways for his Kingdom purposes, but we must be willing to accept his grace.

The sin of Adam and Eve created chaos in that which was perfect order. The Garden of Eden was a place where Adam and Eve had direct communication with God, and were provided with their every physical and spiritual need. When they disobeyed God, sin entered the world which caused chaos in their lives and in ours. But, when Jesus came, he made a way for us to be with God again. Through his blood, by dying on the cross and rising again, he made a way for God's order to reign over us, once again. In Heaven we will experience a perfect order and fellowship with Jesus that is God ordained.

> 'He will wipe every tear from their eyes. There will be no more death' or mourning or crying or pain, for the old order of things has passed away. (Revelation 21:4)

On this side of heaven, let us strive to bring order to our little corners of creation, our homes. Let us strive to love and serve our spouses. Let us attempt to care for and train up our children according to Biblical standards. Let us represent Jesus well!

## Ways to Bring Order to Chaos in Your Home and Heart:

- Make the bed.
- When you don't know what to do, clean the dishes in the sink.

- Establish a cleaning schedule.

- Meal plan.

- Give yourself one day of the week that you are going to do nothing in terms of housework.

- Join a Bible Study. It is such a blessing to be able to study God's Word, and to have Christian women hold you accountable.

- Pray out loud in your car.

- Listen to Christian music.

- Smile more often! :)

- Ask for the Lord's forgiveness each day.

> *But who can discern their own errors?*
> *Forgive my hidden faults.*
> *Keep your servant also from willful sins;*
> *may they not rule over me.*
> *Then I will be blameless,*
> *innocent of great transgression.*
> *May these words of my mouth and this meditation of my heart*
> *be pleasing in your sight,*
> *Lord, my Rock and my Redeemer.*
> *Psalm 19:12-14*

- Pray for wisdom.

> *If any of you lacks wisdom, you should ask God, who gives generously to all without finding fault, and it will be given to you. James 1:5*

- Pray for your children's Salvation.

- Pray for protection over your husband's heart and mind.

- Do good.

> *Trust in the Lord and do good; dwell in the land and enjoy safe pasture. Take delight in the Lord, and he will give you the desires of your heart. Psalm 37:3-4*

• Choose what is right.

> *For the Lord God is a sun and shield;*
> *the Lord bestows favor and honor;*
> *no good thing does he withhold*
> *from those whose walk is blameless. Psalm 84:11*

*Dear Jesus,*

*Thank you for establishing order in the midst of this cha-otic, crazy, sinful world. Thank you for making a way that we might have eternal life with you someday. Thank you God for divinely creating us, and for orchestrating our lives perfectly, according to your plan. Thank you for your faithfulness in systematically writing our stories. Give us strength and endurance to run this race in such a way that we might receive a crown of glory. Help us to be godly wives and mothers who grace our homes and the world around us. In Jesus' heavenly name we pray, amen.*

## Steps of Faith:

• Add an item to the list of "Ways to Bring Order to Chaos in Your Home and Heart." Maybe it is a goal, or maybe it is something that you are already doing and need to stay mind-ful of and continue practicing.

# Chapter 5

# Presence

"The days are long, but the years are short."

—Gretchen Rubin

The other day, we celebrated my little boy's first birthday. He had a "Baby Shark" cake equipped with bright blue icing, a little king's crown party hat with a number one on it, a banner that had a photo for each month of his first year, and a Mickey Mouse balloon. I don't even know how it happened. It's like I blinked and we were all singing "The Happy Birthday Song" to him for the first time. He is still very much a baby, but now a one year old.

If you were to ask me how we were doing on an ordinary day, six months prior, my answer to you probably would have been, "we're exhausted." When you have a new baby, your world gets turned upside down and you wonder if life will ever be the same, or even remotely similar to what it was like before the baby was born. The answer to this wondering is a resounding *no*, life will never be the same; but it can be even better.

Your baby is not always going to need you to change his diapers. He is not always going to need you to brush his teeth, give him a bath, or even to put his clothes on. Eventually he is going to do these things himself. I know as a young mom, it might not seem like there is a light at the end of the tunnel at times, but I am here to tell you there is!

My father in law recently told me a story of a "long ago" episode that happened when their youngest son, Patrick was about three and a half:

> I was attempting to dress him for church when he announced, "I'm big enough to put my clothes on myself." Being in a hurry, I replied, "I know you are, but Daddy likes to help you." Immediately he acquiesced, saying "That's okay, because someday I'll have to help you get dressed." The hair on my neck stood up.

The other day, Emma Claire snatched her toothbrush from me and insisted upon brushing her own teeth. Later that week, she put both of her boots on her feet. The left was on the right, and vice versa, but I was impressed. A few days later, she grabbed her diminutive hairbrush and attempted to brush her own hair. The bristles were facing away from her head, but in that precious moment, all of the puzzle pieces started falling into place and I began to realize how quickly babies grow up and become independent little people. We must strive to be present in their lives each day, both mentally and physically orelse we run the risk of missing out on all of the little unexpected joys that happen along the way.

The next thing I know, Emma Claire will be walking across a stage receiving a diploma. One day she will say "I do," and this is overwhelming to my young mama heart. Right now it feels like she is going to be in diapers forever and is always going to shun the potty like she is currently doing, but I know this is simply not true. Eventually she will get potty trained (everyone does.) Someday she will graduate from high school and go off to college. Some beautiful day she will get married to the love of her life and start a family of her own. This honestly makes me want to hyperventilate and gives me all the feels. But it is also reassuring, because this is God's plan.

Your presence as a mama is crucial to your little baby's heart. They may not say it often, but they love you dearly. They may not know how to put it into words, but they need you. They may not state it, but they love it when you get down on the floor and play with them. They may only realize it subliminally, but they love it when you sing to them. They love your voice. Their hearts are warmed by your "I love yous." They may not draw it to your attention, but they desperately need yours.

Did you know that we are teaching our children about the nature of God through our daily interactions with them? That's right, the first glimpse of their Heavenly Father's love is transposed through yours. Love them well! This sets your children up to receive Christ at an early age. It opens doors for your children to be able to love others and establish healthy, secure relationships as adults.

When you are present in your children's lives, teaching them right from wrong, and enabling them to grow, you are speaking volumes about God's love. God loves you and wants your relationship with him to be firmly established. Our children long for this same type of security. They need present parents to help them succeed and feel loved, which gives them confidence.

## Relationship Evaluation

Are you confident in your relationship with your child? Be honest, on a scale from one to ten, what number would you choose to rate your level of confidence? How can you gain the difference between your number in order to reach ten?

Do you need to set a timer and vow to not be on your phone for a half hour in the evenings, and simply play with your kids? Do you need to say no to a few commitments that are pushing both you and your kids past your limits? Should you be incorporating Christ more in your daily conversations with your children? Could you pray with them more often? Could you be a little more concerned with the state of their hearts rather than their outward behavior? I know that I could personally do all of these things and have better relationships with my children. I encourage you to come alongside me and do the same.

## Choosing the Presence of Jesus

Think about how much you love your children. The Lord loves you with this same kind of fierce, beautiful, unconditional love times infinity. His love for you and for your children is comparable to a mother or a father's love, but it is amplified to an extent that we cannot even fathom.

I love the analogy of a mother's love being like that of my Heavenly Father's, but honestly it does not even compare. Jesus loves us infinitely. No only did he die for us, but he was tortured to death when he had immediate access to angels who would come to his rescue and take him off the cross and into Heaven at his beckoned call. Still, he endured the pain. His love for us is so great, and for that I am eternally grateful.

> But Martha was distracted by all the preparations that had to be made. She came to him and asked, "Lord, don't you care that my sister has left me to do the work by myself? Tell her to help me!"

> "Martha, Martha," the Lord answered, "you are worried and upset about many things, but few things are needed— or indeed only one. Mary has chosen what is better, and it will not be taken away from her." Luke 10:40-42

Jesus' love for me makes me want to sit at his feet and be in his presence. Like the story of Mary and Martha, I want to be a modern day Mary and place Jesus above all else. But there are so many distractions that pull me away from the presence of Christ. My phone, computer, the dishes, the laundry, the empty dog bowl, there are so many things. Even so, we are called to take up our crosses daily and follow the Lord.

> Then he said to them all: "Whoever wants to be my disciple must deny themselves and take up their cross daily and follow me. Luke 9:23

We must deny ourselves of our creature comforts in order to choose Christ. It is a choice. Just like Mary who "chose" what was better, we must choose Jesus, time spent in his Word and prayer before our to-do lists.

> *Dear Jesus,*
>
> *I love you. Please help me to prioritize you. Thank you for my children and for your plan for their lives. I trust you with my children, Lord. I surrender my control over them to you God. Help me to be a kind, loving, present mom in their lives each day. In Jesus' name I pray, amen.*

## Steps of Faith:

- Put your phone down and interact with your children for thirty minutes today.
- Come and sit at the feet of Jesus. Choose time spent in the Word before your to-do list today.

Chapter 6

# Eat Your Fruit

*But the fruit of the Spirit is love, joy, peace, forbearance, kindness, goodness, faithfulness, gentleness and self-control. Against such things there is no law.*

*Galatians 5:22-23*

"Eat your blueberries Emma Claire." I repeated these words to my little girl to no avail. She would not touch the berries. Frustration welled up inside of me, as I took a deep breath and finished preparing the gourmet meal of Kraft Macaroni and Cheese.

She never did eat her blueberries, but in practicing patience and self control, I believe the Lord was able to cultivate something beautiful within my heart through this ordinary interaction. Being a mother can present trying moments in time. It's what we choose to do in those moments that matters. Do we choose to model the Fruits of the Spirit or do we cave to our own flesh instincts and desires?

Being a mom requires patience. In fact, it requires all of the fruits of the Spirit. Being a mom can help you cultivate these traits within yourself if you let motherhood refine you through Christ. By seeking Jesus, acknowledging, and speaking to him throughout the day, we are better equipped to mother with these fruits overflowing out of the wellsprings of our hearts and pouring over into our daily lives.

## Love

Love is a precious, beautiful thing. It comes in various forms, Eros, romantic love, Agape, selfless, unconditional love, and Philos, friendship love. After studying love, I have found that love actually has way more than three facets, but we are going to focus on love in its most powerful form, God's love.

> Dear friends, let us love one another, for love comes from God. Everyone who loves has been born of God and knows God. Whoever does not love does not know God, because God is love. 1 John 4:7-8

> And so we know and rely on the love God has for us. God is love. Whoever lives in love lives in God, and God in them. 1 John 4:16

Being a mom requires us to pour out our love daily. Therefore, we must "rely on the love God has for us" to fill our hearts. If we glean from the love of God each day, through His Word and prayer we are going to be better able to love our children.

Children learn by example. Although we may teach them scripture and listen to "This Little Light of Mine" all day long, if we do not draw from the well of God's love each day, our children are not going to witness the Lord's love in action. We must live lives of love, and because we are flawed creations incapable of loving perfectly, we must rely on God's flawless love to perfect us.

> If I speak in the tongues of men or of angels, but do not have love, I am only a resounding gong or a clanging cymbal. 1 Corinthians 13:1

## Joy

Out of all the people in the world, children are the most joyful creatures that I know of. Their zeal for life is astonishing. Their glee is mesmerizing. Their exuberance is exhilarating. Their jubilation is triumphant. Their innocent, pure joy is in a word, *beautiful.*

We need to take notes from our children and become joyful people who are content with their life circumstances once again. Trust in the Lord is a major part of being content. If we trust in Jesus to provide for our every need, we are going to realize that we have got it made because Jesus is taking care of us. He always has and always will. This is a reason for joy in and of itself. The Lord God is our provider. He knows the plans he has for us, to prosper and not to harm, to give us hope and a future (Jeremiah 29:11).

Even when life feels dark, drab, and lonely, we can draw from our source of strength, the Bible, to acquire joy, and trust in the Lord's provision for our future. Based on God's history of faithfulness, we know that we do not experience pain without a purpose. There is a bigger picture. Though we may walk through painful moments and parts of life, the final destination is green pastures and quiet streams (Psalm 23). God is working behind the scenes in our lives, orchestrating something holy and glorifying to his name.

Life is not always happy, but because we have the hope of Jesus and eternal life someday, we have a reason to be joyful. We must share this reason with the world. Sharing the Good News of the Gospel starts in our homes.

## Peace

The COVID-19 pandemic affected people's mental health dramatically. In 2019, one in ten adults reported symptoms of anxiety or depression, while in 2021 four out of ten adults reported these same symptoms.

Whether this heightened anxiety was caused by fear of the pandemic or isolation, I know that both fear and isolation are enemy tactics. Satan loves to get people alone, subject to their own thoughts, which if we're honest can get a little out of control at times. He loves to establish fear in the minds of people and cause them to think and act irrationally sinful.

Sisters in Christ, we must fight against these enemy tactics! We must band together and establish parameters to keep the enemy at bay. Having a community of believers surrounding you through a church group or women's Bible study is a great defense tactic against isolation. I am a part of a women's Bible study that meets once a week to study God's Word. Having a group of women to hold me accountable to read the Bible has been such a blessing in my life. But, as a mom, this is something that I have to prioritize. Time spent in God's Word does not just happen. I have to use my spare time wisely. I read the Bible typically at naptime, but sometimes in the evenings after my kids go to bed. My women's Bible study meets every Wednesday at 8 PM virtually through Facebook Live Chat. This is a perfect time for most of the moms to meet because it is after bedtime. We are a band of like minded ladies who are mostly mothers going through similar struggles and life circumstances. We open up to each other and pray for each other weekly. I love what one of the ladies in the group shared recently. She said something to the effect of, "I feel like I can open up and share my heart with you ladies liberally, because I believe that the prayers of the righteous are heard by God."

> *Therefore confess your sins to each other and pray for each other so that you may be healed. The prayer of a righteous person is powerful and effective. James 5:16*

I encourage you to find a group of women that will spur you on to get into God's Word and to live for Jesus. There is so much godly wisdom to glean from others who know and love Christ. Accountability is key when it comes to a thriving relationship with the Lord.

> *And let us consider how we may spur one another toward love and good deeds, not giving up meeting together, as some are in the habit of doing, but encouraging one*

*another—and all the more as you see the Day approaching. Hebrews 10:24-25*

## Patience

Patience . . . where to begin! Patience is essential when it comes to being a kind-hearted, loving mother. But, I cannot help but wonder if there is a deeper, Biblical connotation to patience in motherhood that delves beyond refraining one's temper.

> *Jesus continued: "There was a man who had two sons. The younger one said to his father, 'Father, give me my share of the estate.' So he divided his property between them.*
>
> *"Not long after that, the younger son got together all he had, set off for a distant country and there squandered his wealth in wild living. After he had spent everything, there was a severe famine in that whole country, and he began to be in need. So he went and hired himself out to a citizen of that country, who sent him to his fields to feed pigs. He longed to fill his stomach with the pods that the pigs were eating, but no one gave him anything.*
>
> *"When he came to his senses, he said, 'How many of my father's hired servants have food to spare, and here I am starving to death! I will set out and go back to my father and say to him: Father, I have sinned against heaven and against you. I am no longer worthy to be called your son; make me like one of your hired servants.' So he got up and went to his father.*
>
> *"But while he was still a long way off, his father saw him and was filled with compassion for him; he ran to his son, threw his arms around him and kissed him. Luke 15:11-20*

Our children are going to disappoint us. It's our reaction to their sin that matters. We can be focused on making our children behave like little toy soldiers, or we can be concerned with the well-being of their hearts. Training a child so that they recognize the heart issue of their sin, versus an "I'm sorry because I got caught" mentality is of much greater value. We do this through compassion and understanding. This does not mean to spare the rod or give your child a pardon, but it does mean to approach disciplining a child with self control and the heart of God in mind.

The Saturday night before we dedicated our children to the Lord, the pastor of our church held a dinner in which wise counsel was provided to the parents. The children's pastor told us a story that awakened something inside of me. She revealed how she had always been so concerned about the Salvation of her children. She did everything she could do to immerse them in the knowledge and love of Jesus; church every Sunday, Bible camps, youth group, etc. One Wednesday evening her son stated that he did not want to go to the youth group. This pattern continued over the course of the next several weeks. Finally, Cynthia and her husband sat down and had a conversation with their son to get to the heart of the matter. "The truth is, I don't know if I believe in Jesus anymore," he confessed. This was earth shattering, heart breaking news to both Cynthia and her husband. "Well I hope you don't die tonight," was Cynthia's quick, emotional response. She immediately regretted her words.

Eventually, their son decided he did believe in Jesus. He recommitted his life to Christ and his parents were overjoyed. But during those few weeks of doubt, their hearts were in shambles. They sought the Lord fervently during that time, and it's no secret that the Lord answered their prayers and brought their prodigal son back to Jesus.

Our children are not always going to make wise decisions. They will sometimes be led astray. We need to hold tight to our faith in their Salvation and be avid prayer warriors, lifting up our children to the Lord, daily.

I'm not saying that if your child does not want to go to church or youth group to allow them not to go. You are the parent. What I am saying is that it is a long road. Just like you made mistakes along the way, your kids will too. Allow them to learn from their mistakes, and do not shelter them from the consequences, but provide them godly counsel and wisdom in their every season.

Godly patience is a lifelong fruit of the Spirit that we will need to cultivate, water, and deroot weeds from at times. Eventually, we will get to watch beautiful flowers bud within the hearts and throughout the lives of our children because of our diligence in loving, correcting, and forgiving them.

*But the seed on good soil stands for those with a noble and good heart, who hear the word, retain it, and by persevering produce a crop. Luke 8:15*

## Kindness

*She opens her mouth with wisdom,*
*and the teaching of kindness is on her tongue.*
*Proverbs 31:26 (ESV)*

My mom is one of the kindest people that I know. She is constantly pouring herself out by taking care of her grandkids, throwing her friends' daughters baby showers, hosting wedding showers, birthday parties, and more. She is pleased to plan family vacations. She mails me cute clothes for my children to wear, upon occasion. She is such a wonderful mom and grandmother.

Beyond the showers, parties, trips, and other externals, my mom refuses to speak poorly about others. To their face, or behind their back, my mom simply does not partake in gossip or slander. This is something I admire greatly about my mom. I wish to be more like her in many ways, but especially when it comes to being generous and speaking kind words about others.

## Goodness

*Be kind and compassionate to one another, forgiving each other, just as in Christ God forgave you. Ephesians 4:32*

Forgiving others quickly, fully, and repetitively is what we are called to do as mothers; especially when it comes to our spouses, children, and family members. A mark of God's goodness growing in our lives is the ability to forgive.

Forgiveness will set you free. It will take years off of your age, bring joy to your heart, and enable the fruits of the Spirit to thrive in your heart and daily life. Forgiveness is what the Lord calls us to as believers and followers of Christ.

> *Then Peter came to Jesus and asked, "Lord, how many times shall I forgive my brother or sister who sins against me? Up to seven times?" Jesus answered, "I tell you, not seven times, but seventy-seven times. Matthew 18:21-22*

## Faithfulness

> *No temptation has overtaken you except what is common to mankind. And God is faithful; he will not let you be tempted beyond what you can bear. But when you are tempted, he will also provide a way out so that you can endure it. 1 Corinthians 10:13*

In the same way that God was, is, and always will be faithful to us, we too must lead faithful lives, and choose to do what is right. Is it going to be easy? No! Notice the words, "No sin has overtaken you" in 1 Corinthians 10:13. Sin doesn't gently knock on the doors of our lives. It storms in, busting down doors and shattering windows. It takes over. However, once the match is lit and flames begin to consume the place, the Lord provides a way out. We will be tempted to sin, but there is a choice. Sometimes we must prayerfully look for the escape route, but it is always there.

Let us live for Christ and choose to escape the heat of the moment when life scenarios and thoughts entice us to sin. Let us faithfully endure in doing and choosing what Jesus would do on any given day. We have the power of Christ alive in us! We have the power to practice self control, and make faith filled choices, even when our flesh rages against it.

## Gentleness

*Remind the people to be subject to rulers and authorities, to be obedient, to be ready to do whatever is good, to slander no one, to be peaceable and considerate, and always to be gentle toward everyone. Titus 3:1-2*

The very beginning of the book of Titus, written by Paul, begins with a reminder to be gentle. Paul compares gentleness to the acts of obedience, doing good, slandering no one, being peaceable and considerate. These facets all fall under the umbrella of godly gentleness.

How can we be obedient? As Christ followers we must strive to be obedient to the Lord God. As wives we can be submissive to our husbands. I just visualized many of you ladies cringing at my mention of the "S" word, but so often the word submissive is misinterpreted. As gentle women, we are to imitate Christ's humility.

*Do everything without grumbling or arguing, so that you may become blameless and pure, "children of God without fault in a warped and crooked generation." Then you will shine among them like stars in the sky. Philippians 2:14-15*

Philippians 2:14 calls us to not argue or complain. As a woman, this can be hard to do. There are many things that do not fall in line with my vision as an order-bringing, nurture-giving creation. Therefore, my natural tendency is to complain. However, as Christ followers we are called not to argue or complain. This includes when our husbands ask us to do something. This includes unloading the dishwasher. This includes cleaning the floors. This even includes the ever growing mountain of dirty laundry. When our husbands come home from work and ask us about our day, we need to be wives who are able to point out the positive. Instead of having a nagging, complaining, or argumentative attitude, we need to be graceful. In this way, we can shine as wives and our children will have a gentle, role model of a mother to look up to.

## Self Control

> *Likewise, teach the older women to be reverent in the way*
> *they live, not to be slanderers or addicted to much wine,*
> *but to teach what is good. Then they can urge the younger*
> *women to love their husbands and children, to be self-*
> *controlled and pure, to be busy at home, to be kind, and to*
> *be subject to their husbands, so that no one will malign the*
> *word of God. Titus 2:3-5*

I love this series of verses found in Titus chapter 2. As women
of God, we are called to live pure lives. This entails not drinking
too much wine, not gossipping, teaching and influencing others
by the way we conduct our lives in a godly way. We are called to
encourage and inspire younger women to love their husbands and
children with all their might, to be self-controlled with our words
and actions, and to maintain purity of our hearts and minds.
Godly women are to be hardworking, kind, and good nurturers
and providers at home. Women of faith are to be "subject to their
husbands" by being respectful, and by letting their spouses lead.
All of this is to be in effect so that people do not malign, hate,
despise, misinterpret, or reject the Word of God.

May the Fruits of the Spirit culminate in your life so that people accept the Gospel message as truth and dedicate their lives to
Christ. Influence the world in a godly way. Live for Christ through
love, joy, peace, patience, kindness, goodness, faithfulness, gentleness, and self control. Your life will be abundant and you will grace
the world around you with your fruit. Your children will be edified
because of your godly living. They will be inspired because of God's
Truth present in your life that is available to them. Your family will
hunger and thirst for righteousness, and will in turn call you blessed.

## Steps of Faith:

- Zoom in on one Fruit of the Spirit that you want to cultivate in your life? Love, joy, peace, patience, kindness, goodness, faithfulness, gentleness, and self control. Pick one, and
  prayerfully practice weaving its attributes into your daily life.

Chapter 7

# Strong Mom

*She is clothed with strength and dignity;*
*she can laugh at the days to come.*

Proverbs 31:25

I didn't know her name or have any connections to her, but she knelt down by me, and helped me clean up my daughter's throw up with baby wipes from her car. She had a child of her own with her. We were just outside the Mother's Day Out entrance when Emma Claire suddenly lost her cookies and began throwing up everywhere. I was horrified, worried about Emma, and slightly embarrassed all at the same time. I began changing Emma into her extra outfit tucked away in her backpack, (the one I thought I would never have to access,) wiping off the throw up as best I could with my bare hands, when this kind hearted mother approached me asking how she could help. She happened to have baby wipes in her car and volunteered those as tribute to the cause. I was beyond grateful for her help.

Many other moms passed us by in what was most likely a combination of disgust and sympathy. It was truly gross, and I have to say that I would have probably been one of those mothers side stepping the situation before kneeling down to help. It reminded me of the Bible story The Good Samaritan. Here was this mother with enough on her plate already, taking care of her own child, brave and strong enough to help a lowly puke covered mother like me. I didn't deserve her help, but she reminded me of Jesus that day.

How can we remind others of Jesus? Through generous donations, letters of encouragement, and prayer, certainly. But, I think there is an even more meaningful way.

> When he had finished washing their feet, he put on his clothes and returned to his place. "Do you understand what I have done for you?" he asked them. "You call me 'Teacher' and 'Lord,' and rightly so, for that is what I am. Now that I, your Lord and Teacher, have washed your feet, you also should wash one another's feet. I have set you an example that you should do as I have done for you. John 13:12-15

If we got down on our hands and knees in the moment to wash our neighbor's feet and met whatever immediate need they had, or bound up a stranger's obvious, seeping heart wound that needed urgent attention and care, or stopped our busy lives long enough to notice the lonely person standing by themselves at the street corner, maybe those people's hearts would scoot a little bit closer to Jesus. If we made eye contact, walked over, conversed with and encouraged that person on the street corner before handing them a few dollars and a Bible, maybe they would actually open it. I can see Jesus' fingerprints all over these types of scenarios.

Loving in the moment has the greatest potential to impact others in a significant, heart changing way. We need to be on the lookout for others in our everyday, ordinary, busy lives. "Busy" is just an excuse for the fact that something else is prioritizing our time and attention. We need to pay attention to the world around us, because there is always a need. There are constant, urgent matters occuring every day that require us to get out of our own little worlds in order to help. In the name of Jesus, because this is what he has called us to do, let us love others in the everyday moments of our ordinary lives. This is how we can live extraordinary lives for Christ and be the Salt of the Earth.

*"You are the salt of the earth. But if the salt loses its salti-
ness, how can it be made salty again? It is no longer good
for anything, except to be thrown out and trampled under-
foot. Matthew 5:13*

## Motherhood Is Not Always Easy

The book of Job found in the Bible is about a wealthy man who
God allowed to be tested through trials and afflictions. Job was
considered blameless in the eyes of the Lord, "a man of complete
integrity" (Job 1:8). The Lord was confident that Job would remain faithful, even in the face of adversity. For the glory of God,
Job was tested.

> *What I feared has come upon me;*
> *what I dreaded has happened to me. Job 3:25*

Through a series of terrible tribulations, Job remained faithful to the Lord. He experienced the mass slaughter of his livestock, the horrific violent death of his sons and daughters, the
demise of his health, and many more hardships. Job's life was full
of grief. Terrible news struck all at once, like the explosion of a
massive load of dynamite. In the blink of an eye his world had
come to ruins. Although he was grief stricken and perpetually
asked the Lord, "Why?" he continued to praise and acknowledge
God, through it all. In the end, the Lord blessed Job with twice as
much as he had before (Job 42:10).

> *The Lord blessed the latter part of Job's life more than the*
> *former part. He had fourteen thousand sheep, six thou-*
> *sand camels, a thousand yoke of oxen and a thousand*
> *donkeys. Job 42:12*

Motherhood is not always peaches, roses, and ice cream
cones. It is full of hardship and tribulation. Each day we are faced
with struggles both great and small. Similar to children who have
tendencies to make mountains out of what we would consider
molehills, being a mom presents weekly trials that may seem

small in the long run, but are major roadblocks in the day to day. We have to trust that God is going to provide and deliver. We may sometimes feel stretched in our abilities and capabilities as mothers, but we have to trust in God's provision. We must trust God's timing. We have to default to our knowledge of God's goodness. Based on His Word, and history of faithfulness in our lives, we know that we serve a good Father. We can rely on his strategic plans that are *for* us.

Revisit a time in your past that the Lord delivered you from a certain form of captivity. It may have been a trial, a spiritual attack, the death of a loved one, a broken relationship, or an unhealthy thought process. In what way has God delivered you in the past and shown his character of faithfulness in your life?

_____

_____

_____

_____

_____

_____

*Consider it pure joy, my brothers and sisters, whenever you face trials of many kinds, because you know that the testing of your faith produces perseverance. Let perseverance finish its work so that you may be mature and complete, not lacking anything. James 1:2-4*

We have to be strong moms, able to weather life's storms. Through the thick and thin moments of motherhood, we must trust in the Lord in the strength of his might (Ephesians 6:10). Motherhood is going to rock us and therefore, we must establish a firm foundation on the Rock, the Lord God, Jesus Christ as our Savior and daily strength.

I remember getting a stomach bug at the beginning of the year, and being so sick. I was in need of rest, gatorade, and a toilet nearby. The next morning I was extremely dehydrated, had a splitting headache, and still felt a little queasy. My husband assumed that I would be better in the morning and was exhausted from taking care of the kids by himself. "I am going to need your help with the kids today," he told me desperately. I had to rally! I drank some gatorade, ate some chicken noodle soup for lunch, and was as present as possible throughout the day.

Sometimes trials are physical, but other times trials exist in the spiritual, ongoing battles in our hearts and minds; or situational, through financial affliction, or circumstantial division. In whatever way we struggle, the common thread for us as mothers is that we do not have the luxury of checking out or giving in to the chaos of the storm. We must fight to be present, joyful, and peaceful on a day to day basis for our children's sake. They need us. Therefore, we must rely on Christ to weather life's storms.

Studying God's Word is a great tool that we can use to combat the enemy through trials and afflictions. We can lean in on the Lord through prayer. We can ask those who know and love Jesus to pray for us. Even though we may feel like checking out and putting out the "Do Not Disturb" sign when life gets tough, for our children's sake we must maintain a mindset of Christ, a spirit of joy, a heart of thanksgiving, a demeanor of holiness, and a lifestyle of God's love.

*Dear Jesus,*

*We pray for your presence in our lives. Forgive us when we fail to rely on your wisdom and strength and walk according to our own ways. Help us to fully rely on you, God. May we depend on your life giving, holy presence each day. In Jesus' everlasting name we pray, amen.*

Steps of Faith:

- In what way can you be a strong mom today? Is it calling your grandmother even though your free time is limited? Is it helping throw a baby shower for your friend or cousin who is newly pregnant? Could it be volunteering to help watch your friend's children while they are moving? In what way can you go above and beyond in being a mom and friend through loving others?

## Chapter 8

# The Art of Tightrope Walking

Tightrope walkers have always fascinated me. Their mental strength and ability to fight against nature itself is astounding. The key to tightrope walking is effectively maintaining your center of mass directly over the rope. This can be done more readily with bent, slightly bowed knees, because the closer you are to the rope the harder it is to fall. Imagine a tall, slender vase versus a short, stout one. The short, stout one is going to be more difficult to knock over when the same force is applied to both vases.

In this same way, there are precautions that we need to take and heart adjustments we need to make each and every day in order to walk more closely with Christ. Our natural nature and tendency is sin. We must focus and recenter our lives on Christ in order to stay zeroed in on living for Jesus and loving others in his name.

Another competing element of tightrope walking is that the natural tendency of the rope or wire is to slightly twist with every step taken. The tightrope walker has to apply what is known as "rotational inertia," or positioning oneself to fight against the rotational force of the rope. This is a hidden element that many people do not realize as spectators, but makes tightrope walking all the more difficult.

As moms, we have daily external struggles and challenges; laundry, the dishes, cooking dinner, cleaning the house, picking up toys, feeding the kids, and many more "to-do's." Maintaining a lifestyle of balance and not becoming mentally overwhelmed used to be a huge challenge for me personally. It made me a very snappy, rushed person, unable to offer my presence in full, or enjoy God's peace in my life. My life was like a ticking clock, revolving around my daily external duties, while inside my heart was crying out for Jesus. It wasn't until one of my best friends invited me to be a part of her women's Bible study that the vicious cycle was broken. I began to get into God's Word and the Lord softened my heart and enabled me to realize that although my housework chores were being checked off in stride, inside I was totally broken and in need of the presence of Jesus to rejuvenate my weary soul. As I focused more of my time in God's Word and committed myself to daily prayer my anxiousness subsided and I was able to go about living with the peace of God's presence alive and flourishing in me.

As moms, we build up these ideas in our minds that we have to be perfect, each and every day. We push ourselves to our breaking points in terms of performance as mothers and wives. We overload our schedules and underfeed our souls. This is simply not the way we are meant to live our lives. It is okay to smell the roses and realize God's goodness, and spend time with him every day. In fact, it is good. Time spent with the Lord is not a chore, but rather a blessing and priority we get to experience daily as Christ followers. However, we do have to make time for God, and leave some margin in our lives in order for this to be possible. If we try to carry too much while walking across the tightrope of our lives, then we will be unable to achieve balance.

*And Jesus grew in wisdom and stature, and in favor with*
*God and man. Luke 2:52*

Jesus was the master tightrope walker when it came to a godly sense of balance. He grew in four distinct areas, wisdom, (which comes from reading and applying God's Word,) stature, (physical fitness,) in favor with God, (Jesus conversed daily with the Father and lived to please the Lord,) and man, (Jesus was a disciple maker and friend.) As Christ followers, we are called to develop our lives in these same four areas.

God's Word encourages and inspires us to be more like Jesus. If you are not currently in God's Word consistently, I encourage you to do so. But, might I warn you; it will change you. It will change the way you think and act. It might even get in the way of you accomplishing every single task on your to do list. The Word of God will well up inside of you and convict you to apologize and seek God's forgiveness for things you could have otherwise easily concealed. It will tug on your heart and ask you to help when you see a mother kneeling down on the sidewalk with her daughter covered in bodily fluids. It will inspire you to encourage that mom in the checkout line at the grocery store whose child is throwing a hysterical temper tantrum. God's Word will change you, and it may not be convenient or comfortable, but it will be rewarding. You might not win the lottery, get a raise, or experience the sudden heart change of that family member you have been fervently praying for, but God notices your diligence when you love and live from his Word. He is storing up for you treasures in Heaven.

> "Do not store up for yourselves treasures on earth, where moths and vermin destroy, and where thieves break in and steal. But store up for yourselves treasures in heaven, where moths and vermin do not destroy, and where thieves do not break in and steal. For where your treasure is, there your heart will be also." Matthew 6:19-21

We need to be more concerned with the eternal and internal conditions of our hearts rather than our external appearances. Facebook and Instagram lie like dogs in terms of representing real life and what really matters to Jesus. A recent study reported that one in three teen girls have escalated body image issues because of Instagram. The study suggested that there are connections between Instagram and teen anxiety and depression. Having a little girl, this breaks my mama heart! It makes me want to closely monitor my kids' screens when they are older. Although these statistics are for teens, I cannot help but realize that Facebook and Instagram most certainly have had these same detrimental effects on some moms.

Before you start scrolling through Facebook or Instagram, I encourage you to download and read the "First Five" app. It is an app created by Proverbs 31 Ministries that provides a five minute daily devotional and reading from God's Word. We need to be doing things that fill us and not drain us as mothers. We need to edify our hearts and minds daily.

> *Do not conform to the pattern of this world, but be transformed by the renewing of your mind. Then you will be able to test and approve what God's will is—his good, pleasing and perfect will. Romans 12:2*

Making heart filling choices with our time in the everyday moments of life is a discipline of a godly woman that we need to adopt! It does not come naturally, but much like tightrope walking, we have to take conscious steps to do things that will fill our cups each day. In this way we can recenter our minds on Christ's likeness and uplift our hearts spiritually and emotionally. The rotational inertia of the tightrope beneath our feet is similar to the world's ability to creep in and tell us what to think, how to feel, and to act on our emotions. We must fight against this oppositional tendency in order to live full lives that are centered on Christ.

> *Dear Jesus,*
>
> *Thank you for your Word. Thank you for your Truth in my life. Thank you for godly women who have come alongside me throughout the course of motherhood to uplift and inspire me. Thank you for strategically planting godly influences in my life. I praise you for your goodness! Please forgive me when I lose my balance in life, and fall off the tightrope in terms of the plans and purposes you have for me. Forgive me and help me to get back up again, each and every time.*
>
> *Help me live for you alone Jesus. Let my life honor and glorify you. Give me determination to choose you in the small things God. Whether it be laundry or your Word,*

*or scrolling verses a daily devotional, give me the discipline and self control to choose you above all else Jesus. I love you Lord. Amen*

## Steps of Faith:

- Make heart filling choices with your time today. Choose to listen to the Christian radio station rather than secular music, or read a Bible Study on your phone before allowing yourself to browse through social media.

Chapter 9

# Mothers of the Bible

B eing a mother is a divinely appointed mission. Look at the life of Eve, Sarah, Rachel, Jochebed, Hannah, and Mary, for example. These women were godly women of faith who bore children who did great things for the Lord. There is much to be learned from the lives of these women. They raised their children up in the knowledge, fear, love, and admonishment of the Lord, and their children's lives were fruitful because of it.

Even on days when it does not feel like it, make no mistake that you are changing the lives of your children, preparing their hearts to receive Christ if they are young, teaching them about Jesus' life and his great love for us. As mothers, we are simply vessels, doing the Lord's will, teaching and helping our children grow closer to Jesus. We are role models and leaders in our homes, and in the hearts of our children.

### Eve

*God blessed them and said to them, "Be fruitful and increase in number; fill the earth and subdue it. Rule over*

*the fish in the sea and the birds in the sky and over every
living creature that moves on the ground." Genesis 1:28*

The Hebrew name for Eve means "giver of life." Eve was the mother
of all the living. She most likely gave birth many many times. She
was fruitful as the Lord ordained.

I have noticed a trend that women all across America are
having less children. The average number of people per household in America in 1960 was 3.67, while the current average is
3.13. This accounts for many reasons, and there is much specula-
tion as to why family sizes are shrinking, but let us not forget that
children are a blessing.

> *Children are a heritage from the Lord,*
> *offspring a reward from him.*
> *Like arrows in the hands of a warrior*
> *are children born in one's youth.*
> *Blessed is the man*
> *whose quiver is full of them.*
> *Psalm 127:3-5*

Are children a lot of work? Yes! Are they totally worth it?
Absolutely! I have two children of my own, and our family is
still growing. This is a conviction of my heart. While my hands
feel full, I know that the Lord has this divine ability to widen the
diameter of all that we can hold when we open up our arms and
hearts to him.

## Sarah

*Abraham and Sarah were already very old, and Sarah was
past the age of childbearing. So Sarah laughed to herself as
she thought, "After I am worn out and my lord is old, will I
now have this pleasure?" Genesis 18:11-12*

There is wisdom to be gleaned from the life of Sarah. Sarah gave
birth to a son, Isaac, in her old age when her husband Abraham
was a hundred years old. At the age of ninety, Abraham received

a promise from God that he would be the father of many nations. This promise caused Sarah to laugh, because she realized her age. But, she knew the Lord was faithful. This promise presented a ten year waiting span for God's provision to unfold, for Isaac to be born. This must have required a lot of patience and trust in the Lord. Like Sarah we must have patience in the Lord's timing, and trust in his provision for our lives.

## Rachel

*When Rachel saw that she was not bearing Jacob any children, she became jealous of her sister. So she said to Jacob, "Give me children, or I'll die!"*

*Jacob became angry with her and said, "Am I in the place of God, who has kept you from having children?" Genesis 30:1-2*

There is much we can learn from the life of Rachel. Rachel was loved and favored by her husband Jacob. She was lovely in form, but that did not prevent her from not being able to bear children for a long time. She grew impatient in her waiting, as so many of us do when we desperately want something. She became jealous of her sister who was able to have many children. At one point she said to Jacob, "Give me children, or I'll die!" Jacob's response was to redirect his wife to the Lord.

In this same way, when things do not go our way, we must seek the Lord and cry out to Jesus. Before expressing an urgent heart matter to our husbands, friends, or even a counselor, we must talk to Jesus first. He is the one able to heal, bless, and wipe away our every tear. He wants to hear from us, first.

When life does not go according to *our* plan, we can trust in God's way and know that *the Lord's* plans are for us. He guides, directs, and goes before us. Sometimes he protects us by not giving us what we want at the moment of our petitioning. In this way, we know that God is good. He is faithful, protective, and has our days planned out perfectly, according to his will.

*Many are the plans in a person's heart,*
*but it is the Lord's purpose that prevails. Proverbs 19:21*

# Jochebed

Jochebed was the mother of Moses, Aaron, and Miriam. She saved Moses from being slaughtered at the time when Pharaoh declared that all Hebrew baby boys be killed upon birth. After three months of hiding her baby, she placed Moses in a papyrus basket that floated along the Nile River until it came to the palace and was noticed by the Egyptian princess who had compassion for the child and raised the baby as her own. Moses grew up to be a man of God, appointed to lead the Israelites out of slavery.

Jochebed was a brave mother. She was able to let her child go, in order to save him. She did what was best for her child, even though letting go had to have been so incredibly tough. We are called to do what is best for our children, even when it is uncomfortable or emotionally difficult. We are to help our children live their best lives. When it seems like our children are drifting down the dangerous Nile River and Nile Crocodiles are snapping, we must fervently pray, and trust that God knows the way and has a destination in mind for our children's lives.

# Hannah

*In her deep anguish Hannah prayed to the Lord, weeping bitterly. And she made a vow, saying, "Lord Almighty, if you will only look on your servant's misery and remember me, and not forget your servant but give her a son, then I will give him to the Lord for all the days of his life, and no razor will ever be used on his head." 1 Samuel 1:10-11*

I love Hannah's prayer of petition to the Lord for a son. She reveals the cry of her heart to the Lord, and as women of God we are called to do the same. Jesus hears our prayers, notices our tears, and has compassion on us through our afflictions. Motherhood is tough and many tears are shed throughout the course. If we present our heart cries to the Lord he will not only hear us, but also comfort us with his love and assurance. God's Word is our source of Truth to look to when comfort and consolation are needed. The Word of the Lord is alive and active and offers so much grace, love, and wisdom to us through our trials.

The house of the Lord is where Hannah prayed this prayer. What better way to pray than in the presence of the Lord? We do not have to be at church in order for our prayers to be effectively heard. Because of the cross, and Christ's eternal connection to us through his blood, we can speak freely to him, daily. Christ is all ears when we bow our heads and hearts in prayer.

Hannah followed through with her word and gave Samuel to the Lord at an early age (1 Samuel 1:24). I cannot imagine giving my baby to someone else to raise. Even if it was on account of the Lord, this would be difficult beyond what my mommy mind can comprehend. Hannah was faithful to the Lord. She made a promise to God that she meant, and she kept her promise. In this same way, we are to be faithful as mothers in raising up our children in the ways of the Lord, in the best way that we know how. We are to be faithful wives, honest friends, and loving neighbors. We are to be faithful and obedient to God's Word. We are to live holy lives.

Motherhood is a sanctification process where we are given the opportunity to be purified through trials, hardship, tests, and tribulation. While there are many joyful moments in motherhood, there are also many uncomfortable ones that test our faith and call us to rise up to the standard of God's holiness. Righteousness versus sin is a choice that we cannot be triumphant from in and of ourselves. Motherhood requires us to draw from the strength of Jesus to overcome moments of weakness, and to lean in on Christ's love through times of need.

## Mary

*The angel went to her and said, "Greetings, you who are highly favored! The Lord is with you." Luke 1:28*

Mary was just a girl when the Lord appointed her to bear his son. She was most likely 14-16 years old when she gave birth to Jesus. This seems very young to us nowadays, but in Biblical times, this was common. Age is just a number, and I don't know about you, but I certainly feel like I am too young to be raising children of my own at times. There are moments when I doubt my abilities and capabilities as a qualified mom, but the Lord does not use the "qualified" but those he calls. We have been called to be mothers. I think the Lord was smiling when he decided to give young women the task of raising children. Jesus infuses us with his strength, and provides us all that we need, each and every day, to help our babies along life's way.

According to the angel Gabriel, Mary was highly favored by the Lord. We know that she was certainly a virgin, but also she must have loved God with all her heart. She was a woman after God's own heart, the chosen mother of God's own son. Mary must have been totally and completely in love with the Lord and was most likely living for him, so that God noticed Mary and appointed her for this divine mission. In this same way, let us live for Jesus. Unlike Mary, we have the Holy Spirit, God with us, each and every day of our lives. Jesus was most likely nearby Mary most of his childhood, but he was not yet alive in her heart. It wasn't until Christ's death and resurrection that Mary was able to experience Jesus in full. The Holy Spirit rained down at Pentecost and this was the exact moment that Mary's life and heart was forever changed.

Do you remember when your life was eternally changed, when you accepted Jesus to be the Lord and Savior of your life? Write about it! Describe this joyous moment, and if applicable, include how your parents encouraged and celebrated with you.

---

---

---

_____

_____

_____

_____

I accepted Jesus into my heart at the age of nine at First Baptist Church in Midland Texas. My parents played a major role in influencing my life for Christ. They took me to "big church" and Sunday school. They placed me in Vacation Bible School. When I was old enough, they put me on a charter bus with my two older brothers that was destined for Kanakuk Kamps, which was one of the greatest childhood influences of my life.

Year after year I went back to Kanakuk during the summers. One year in high school, I stayed for a month! I worked as a counselor at Kanakuk Camps throughout college. Kanakuk was a place where you could know, love, and live for God through sports, arts and crafts, mealtime, and a whole lot of fun. We acknowledged the Lord throughout the day in almost everything we did at Kanakuk. This taught me the essence of prayer and seeking Jesus throughout the day. We learned how to have a "quiet time" with the Lord, and practiced this daily at camp.

I would not have had these life changing experiences at Kanakuk had my parents not have been the catalyst in researching, paying for, and allowing me to go as a young child. They certainly knew when to loosen the reins, and as mothers we must prayerfully determine when and how to allow our kids to develop independence and adopt the love of Christ for themselves. Someday we are not going to be around, and our kids will have to live life on their own and take care of themselves. We must infuse their lives with Jesus, but there comes a point in childhood that we have to start loosening our grip on our children's hearts and allow the Holy Spirit to do the work.

*Dear Jesus,*

*Thank you for godly mothers of the past who have walked before us, who have been recorded in your great Book. Thank you for revealing to us wisdom that can be found woven throughout the motives of their hearts and lives. Help us to seek you first Jesus. Help us to fear you God, and place your opinion of our hearts and lives on the forefront of our minds.*

*Jesus, our desire is to be more like you. Help us to live lives of faith and walk according to your precepts. Strengthen us to be modern day Marys, Jochebeds, Eves, Hannahs, Rachels, and Sarahs in the best ways possible. Thank you for your Word, that we can learn about the lives of these godly mothers through the scriptures. Although they were not without sin, you directed their paths for your glory, and I pray that you direct our lives as well. Lord, guide us according to your plans. Jesus, help us to love and lead our children with your great love. Amen*

## Steps of Faith:

- Get into the Word, read and journal about one of these mothers of the Bible that we have discussed.

- In what way can you be a modern day Mary, Jochebed, Eve, Hannah, Rachel, or Sarah? Could you prayerfully work on having sold out faith in the Lord's plan for your life? In light of Eve, could you have another child, or consider adopting?

# Chapter 10

# God's Yes

We had waited to know the gender this time around throughout the course of the entire pregnancy which made delivery day, "D-Day" as we referred to it, all the more exciting. We went in to be induced, bright eyed and bushy tailed at 4:00 AM. Throughout the morning doctors and nurses came in and out to check on the progress of my labor. My husband napped some, but was so excited that his sleep was limited.

When it came time for me to push, I remember it like it was yesterday. My doctor was cracking jokes and talking about his high school experiences of "back in the day." He was taking his job seriously, but when he goes in to deliver a baby, his nerves cause him to comically rant. Honestly, it puts my nerves at bay somewhat as well. One last push, I could see some commotion, and then heard the most beautiful sound of my newborn baby crying. My husband and I were in shock and disbelief at the doctor's news. I was more audible in my excitement, while the shock factor had a firm grip on my husband's shoulder. He stood there stoic and wide eyed after the doctor announced the gender, for a few moment's time. "It's a boy!" The doctor proclaimed above the high pitched, unmistakable cry of our brand new baby boy.

We had wanted and prayed for a healthy baby, leaving gender out of the equation, but both of us knew that it would be exciting to have a boy and embark on a new adventure of all that boys entail. We already had a little girl who we loved and adored, Emma Claire, only 18 months old at the time. The announcement of a boy brought tears of joy to my eyes. The moment they laid that sweet baby boy upon my chest, my heart was full. We named him "David Josiah;" "David" after his father. He would go by his middle name, "Josiah," which means "the Lord has healed or restored." We both thought it was the perfect name.

Throughout the pregnancy, the waiting process of not knowing whether we were going to have a boy or a girl was nerve wracking at times. We were eager to discover the type of adventure we were about to embark on. I was anxious to plan. We both wanted to know the gender, but even moreso, we knew that it would be so exciting to wait and see what the Lord had in store.

Sometimes we have to wait in life. Whether it be for a husband, a baby, a life dream, or some other blessing in life, waiting refines us. It is a sanctification process in which the Lord is able to strengthen our character and dependence upon him.

The waiting process of life is exciting, but also nerve wracking at times. We want joy in the moment, happiness all the time. We want God to deliver his promises ASAP, and this is simply not the way God works. Whether it be to strengthen our faith, to make us depend on him like never before, or to make the blessing that much more significant in our lives, waiting on the Lord is Biblical.

*Now faith is confidence in what we hope for and assurance about what we do not see. Hebrews 11:1*

While waiting is hard, it is rewarding. Still, it is not guaranteed that you will receive the outcome you were hoping for. The Lord works in mysterious ways. God knows what we need. He is going to bless us in accordance with his divine will. His purposes are for us. God is good, all the time.

Even when life circumstances do not resemble God's goodness, know that he is still moving and working in your life, behind the scenes. If you are looking for a specific, "yes" answer to your prayers, realize that God is going to give you his best "yes," which may look a little different than what you had anticipated.

God's timing is often a little different than our preconceived life plans. As a little girl, I always thought I would find my husband in college, or maybe even high school and get married at age 21, just like my mom. I did not get married until I was 25, and the love of my life, my husband and I met after college. The waiting process was extremely difficult. There were definitely some tears along the way, but eventually the Lord brought my husband and I together and he truly is the man of my dreams. Praise the Lord for his goodness. Praise God for his perfect timing. Had my husband and I met earlier in life, we might have been too immature to have a healthy, godly relationship that led to marriage. God had been preparing me, and my husband's heart, for us to meet at the precise moment that was in accordance with his plan. I am thankful that I did not get married until I was 25. I am so incredibly grateful for my husband.

## Dark Valleys

*Therefore, since we are surrounded by such a great cloud of witnesses, let us throw off everything that hinders and the sin that so easily entangles. And let us run with perseverance the race marked out for us, fixing our eyes on Jesus, the pioneer and perfecter of faith. For the joy set before him he endured the cross, scorning its shame, and sat down at the right hand of the throne of God. Consider him who endured such opposition from sinners, so that you will not grow weary and lose heart. Hebrews 12:1-3*

Jesus is the author and perfecter of our faith. He walked this earth and endured the cross so that we would be encouraged. We can be joyful even when we walk through the darkest of valleys because we know that we have the hope of eternal life in Heaven someday. When we wade through the marshy trenches of life, Christ is right there beside us.

More than one of my close friends has experienced a miscarriage. While I cannot say that I personally have, I know the hammer of grief and devastation a miscarriage brings down upon a family. It hits the mother the hardest, and disables her ability to think clearly because she is simply devastated. Carrying on with life as usual becomes exceedingly difficult, because the new life that was once living and active inside of her is gone. People move on from the incident extremely quickly, but the mother's pace of recovery is much slower. Like a snail compared to a jack rabbit, that is how much longer it takes for the mother to be okay. Still, that baby will always retain a piece of that mama's heart, and she may never fully recover, but slowly learns how to live life once again. God enables her with the strength, endurance, and joy she needs to carry on, each day. Through family, friends, and loved ones coming alongside of her, she is able to breathe the fresh air of life once again. The shade of gray that surrounded her world slowly lifts, and life in full color gradually emerges as women encourage her and she is uplifted by God's Word. Through much prayer, tears, and crying out to the Lord, her life becomes full once again, and she is blessed in other ways that she never saw coming.

When life seems despondent, on days that are gray, reach out to Jesus. He always has his hand extended out, you simply need to take hold. He wants to carry you, and be your strength through life's storms. There are mountain highs and valley lows in life that God wants to guide you through. Seek the Lord through your pain. I promise you it is not without purpose. Still, we may never know the exact reason why bad things happen to us on this side of Heaven, but rest assured, and know that God is mighty to save. The Lord has a plan that is the very best "yes" for your life.

> *"I have told you these things, so that in me you may have peace. In this world you will have trouble. But take heart! I have overcome the world." John 16:33*

*Dear Jesus,*

*Thank you for overcoming the world on my account. Thank you Jesus for saving me, so that I might have the peace of your presence in my daily life. I pray that your peace would consume me, and enable me to live fully for you. Help me to remember Philippians 4:6-7 on days when I feel anxious or discouraged. "Do not worry or be anxious about anything, but in everything, by prayer and petition present your requests to God, and the peace of God which transcends all understanding will guard your heart in Christ Jesus." Thank you for your peace which is all consuming, and reassures me daily.*

*Father, I pray that you would comfort me through life's storms. Help me draw near to you through times of need and moments of desperation. As a mom and wife, help me to live life abundantly for you, realizing that my children and spouse are such a blessing, each and every day. In Jesus' holy name I pray, amen.*

## Steps of Faith:

- Is there a plan of yours, or a mindset that you need to let go of in order for the Lord's best "yes" in your life to blossom? Surrender your ways to Jesus, and allow him to perfect your faith.

Chapter 11

# The Law

*For you are not a true Jew just because you were born of Jewish parents or because you have gone through the ceremony of circumcision. No, a true Jew is one whose heart is right with God. And true circumcision is not merely obeying the letter of the law; rather, it is a change of heart produced by the Spirit. And a person with a changed heart seeks praise from God, not from people. Romans 2:28-29*

Our children are growing up in a confusing day and age, this is no secret. The world shouts, "Be what you want to be! Do what you want to do! Live your best life now!" And it seems exciting. Children and teens are so impressionable. We must have an even stronger approach and teach our kids that there is a better way; one that is grace filled, lawful, holy, and pleasing to the Lord. It fills me with sorrow to know that there are children out there who are being led astray by this wayward world. We cannot change the lives and influences of every single child, but we can impact our own, for Christ's sake.

> *"If anyone causes one of these little ones—those who believe in me—to stumble, it would be better for them to have a large millstone hung around their neck and to be drowned in the depths of the sea." Matthew 18:6*

These are the words of Jesus. We are to lead our children in accordance with the Truths found in God's Word, the Bible. We are to love them fervently, to discipline, to correct, and care for them with the love and leadership of Christ.

In the New Testament, the first five books of the Bible, known as the Torah, are thought to have been written by Moses. These books contain and rely on the Ten Commandments. Although Christ has torn the veil through the cross, and we no longer have to atone for our sins through animal sacrifices, or require a priest mediator, the Old Testament and the Ten Commandments are still meant to refine and sanctify our hearts and change the way we live our lives today.

*"You shall have no other gods before me.*

*"You shall not make for yourself an image in the form of anything in heaven above or on the earth beneath or in the waters below. You shall not bow down to them or worship them; for I, the Lord your God, am a jealous God, punishing the children for the sin of the parents to the third and fourth generation of those who hate me, but showing love to a thousand generations of those who love me and keep my commandments.*

*"You shall not misuse the name of the Lord your God, for the Lord will not hold anyone guiltless who misuses his name.*

*"Remember the Sabbath day by keeping it holy. Six days you shall labor and do all your work, but the seventh day is a sabbath to the Lord your God. On it you shall not do any work, neither you, nor your son or daughter, nor your male or female servant, nor your animals, nor any foreigner residing in your towns. For in six days the Lord made the heavens and the earth, the sea, and all that is in them, but he rested on the seventh day. Therefore the Lord blessed the Sabbath day and made it holy.*

*"Honor your father and your mother, so that you may live long in the land the Lord your God is giving you.*

*"You shall not murder.*

*"You shall not commit adultery.*

*"You shall not steal.*

*"You shall not give false testimony against your neighbor.*

*"You shall not covet your neighbor's house. You shall not covet your neighbor's wife, or his male or female servant, his ox or donkey, or anything that belongs to your neighbor." Exodus 20:3-17*

The Ten Commandments, the Law, was similar to a guardian in that these precepts were meant to watch over the Israelites, and keep them out of danger, physically and spiritually. Until the coming of Christ, the Law was intended to help people live lives free of sin, to provide them with a roadmap to godly living. The Law was a lamp to God's people, leading the way to freedom from the bondage of sin.

> *Before the coming of this faith, we were held in custody under the law, locked up until the faith that was to come would be revealed. So the law was our guardian until Christ came that we might be justified by faith. Now that this faith has come, we are no longer under a guardian. Galatians 3:23-25*

Similar to the Law, we as parents must provide godly parameters to our children so that they will grow up knowing, loving, and living for God at an early age. Knowing right from wrong gives children a sense of confidence and security in their daily living. Similar to the Law no longer being in full control after Jesus brought the Holy Spirit to us, someday our children will no longer be under our care. They will face life on their own, with the Lord God, the presence of Jesus, having full custody over their hearts, minds, and hands. While they are under our care, we must correct them, have meaningful conversations, and be intentional about incorporating Christ and godly precepts into their daily lives. When we notice one of our children's hearts hurting, or being led astray by the world, we must be quick to reign them back in, out of love.

Similar to a shepherd watching over his sheep, we have been given the task to shepherd our children in the fear and love of the Lord. We are called to lead them and guide them with all of our strength and might. When lions and other beasts of the field threaten to attack, we are to put ourselves in the way of this foreseen danger, protecting our sheep. Children are innocent creatures who need our help to navigate through the ways of this damaged, dangerous, deceitful world.

The world shouts, "Live your best life now!" but it forgets to add the precursory statement, "At all costs." It states, "Be what you want to be!" But it does not include the part about how this anticipated satisfaction will actually drain your soul and deplete your joy. It demands, "Do what you want to do!" It does not state the fact that there will be consequences.

> *What good is it for someone to gain the whole world, yet forfeit their soul? Mark 8:36*

There are consequences when we break God's law. There are consequences when we break man's law. There are consequences when children break house rules. There are consequences for sin, and this is God ordained. God punishes those he loves (Hebrews 12:6). In this same way, we are to punish our children when they step outside of God's boundaries. In doing this, we provide our children with safety and a sense of security in knowing right from wrong. Their character is developed through discipline.

> *No discipline seems pleasant at the time, but painful. Later on, however, it produces a harvest of righteousness and peace for those who have been trained by it. Hebrews 12:11*

"To spare the rod is to spoil the child." You may have heard this statement, or a similar variation, based on the Bible verse Proverbs 13:24, "Whoever spares the rod hates their children, but the one who loves their children is careful to discipline them." This equates to the connotation that we are not to spare our children from life's consequences. When children are little, yes, spanking and time-outs may be involved. But when our children grow up and become young adults, we cannot bail them out of troubles they bring upon themselves, because in doing so, we teach them that mommy and daddy are here for them, instead of helping them to realize that, *life is hard, and I must do my best in all ways to live faithfully.* This is sometimes a very hard life lesson to learn. Sometimes this lesson is even harder on the parents watching their children struggle, but in equipping our young adult children through minor hardships, we develop their resilience, character, and dependence on the Lord.

> *Trust in the Lord with all your heart*
> *and lean not on your own understanding;*
> *in all your ways submit to him,*
> *and he will make your paths straight. Proverbs 3:5-6*

When disciplining our children, we should keep the heart of God in mind. Instead of acting emotionally, we must prayerfully correct our children. This is a godly discipline that requires patience and a close walk with the Lord. Let us submit our children to the Lord, and correct them out of love.

Let us teach our children the meaning of Proverbs 3:5-6 through the way we live our lives. Let us acknowledge Christ in all that we do, developing the practice of daily prayer and reading God's Word. Let us pray with our kids and read God's Word to them. Let us lead by example, and weave blessings of truth into their daily lives. These blessings of truth are like valuable jewels that they can have, and carry with them for the rest of their lives.

## Such As These

King David was known for many great things, and was referred to as "a man after God's own heart," but he failed at the task of disciplining his son, Adonijah.

> *His father had never rebuked him by asking, "Why do you behave as you do?" He was also very handsome and was born next after Absalom. 1 Kings 1:6*

This lack of discipline led to Adonijah's demise. He led a rebellion and appointed himself king. He had a band of faithful followers, but when the prophet Nathan caught wind of this news, he urged Bathsheba to approach the king and remind him of his promise to appoint Solomon, her son, as king. The deal was sealed, and King David appointed Solomon king that very day. King Solomon pardoned Adonijah's initial rebellion, but later, when Adonijah asked to marry one of the late King David's former wives, Abishag, in secret attempts to overtake the kingdom through the marriage, King Solomon killed Adonijah.

Adonijah's request was an act of treason, and revealed that he still had rebellious intentions at heart. Sometimes when we discipline our children, telling them to stop what they are doing, they may outwardly oblige but inwardly still be holding on to vengeance in their hearts. That is why we must get to the heart of the matter. When our children mess up and make mistakes that are intentional, we need to approach them with our Bibles, God's Word on our hearts, perhaps even a parable from the life of Jesus. We want something that will break through the defensive parameters they have built up on the inside; because while on the outside they may submit to our correction and act in accordance to our request for outward change, but if their hearts are not repositioned, then we have not truly corrected the underlying issue, which is a matter of the heart.

The issue is that if we are not careful, all of our controlling, and making our children behave like obedient robots will catch up with us, and will eventually backfire. I have seen this happen many times. Teens who were once sweet little Bible study bugs go off to college, and rebel. All of the control, all of the restraint that the parents had over these children while they were still at home, (whether the children felt the oppression or not,) is released when these same teenagers leave their homes. These once little Bible study bugs are confronted with mountain highs and valley lows of peer pressure that they never had to face before life in college and as young working professionals. If adult children are not somewhat equipped with a map and compass as their guide to know how to take the trail that goes around and avoids the mountains, they may attempt to climb and this presents a treacherous fate should they slip and fall.

My parents recently attended the funeral of a family friend of ours who was my babysitter growing up. She is not much older than me actually. She died of drug overdose. It had been an ongoing battle for some time, but eventually she slipped and fell. As parents, we must equip our children with a map, God's Word, the Bible, and a compass, which is the Holy Spirit inside of them, a decision they will have to make for themselves.

What our adult children do with the map we give them is not under our control, but we are called to equip them for life's challenges that are surely to come. It is not the parents' fault, should an adult child choose to climb the mountain anyway, but it is our duty to equip them nonetheless. I know many godly parents who did train their children up in the ways of the Lord, and their children still turned away from God as adults. It is not a guarantee that our children will choose to walk in the ways of the Lord, but we must gear them up through teaching them God's Word and God's Love through Biblical, heartfelt discipline.

Some children will grow up knowing *of* Jesus, and will then choose to rebel as young adults, only to slip, fall, and cry out to Jesus. Let Jesus help them up. Do not attempt to rescue or save them from the pit they have gotten themselves into, but toss them a rope that is godly encouragement and urge them to climb back up, in the name of Jesus.

Jesus saves. Remind them of this truth. Remind them of who they once were as innocent little Bible study bugs. Lead them back to God's Word. Don't push, but gently toss down a rope, a Bible, and Living Water. You can't make them drink it, but make eternal life available to them through your love, mercy, and direct guidance. Clearly, audibly, lovingly remind them of Jesus, who is mighty to save.

If your adult child finds Jesus through hardship and trouble, then let it be so. I know it is painful to watch, and that you too experience their storms. But praise the Lord for his faithfulness in your child's life. Praise God when your babies grow up and find

Jesus for themselves. No matter their age, or the circumstances under which the Holy Spirit's prompting was made clear, praise the Lord. Whenever God begins to tug on a child's heart, allow the Lord to do his holy work, and do not hinder them, "for the kingdom of heaven belongs to such as these." Matthew 19:14

*Dear Jesus,*

*I pray that we would write your laws on our hearts and teach our children your ways. Help us to be godly parents and role models who live out the Truth of God's Word in our everyday lives. Help us to love and honor you through obedience. We love you Lord Jesus. Amen*

Steps of Faith:

- In what way can you follow God's Law more diligently? In being more faithful in disciplining your children? With your thought life? By listening to the tugs of the Holy Spirit on your heart throughout the day? In what way can you walk more closely with the Lord through steadfast obedience?

Chapter 12

# Mirage

A mirage could be explained as, "an optical illusion caused by atmospheric conditions, especially the appearance of a sheet of water in a desert or on a hot road caused by the refraction of light from the sky by heated air."

I was speaking with a mom recently, at a birthday party, and asked her, "How is life with three?" She and her husband had recently had their third child. "Well, it is good. But I wish I had been better prepared mentally, because being outnumbered presents some major challenges." This brought me back to the transition I went through in being a full time Elementary Teacher to a stay at home mom.

When I was a teacher, it felt like I had a lot on my plate, a classroom full of 30 children who were my responsibility to educate and fill with knowledge. Little did I know, being a teacher pales in comparison to being a mom. The difference is that the kids in my class were not my own. They were not my full time responsibility. I was able to call it quits at the end of the day, go home, relax, and have some alone time; (and I *need* my alone time.) When I was a teacher, I could not wait to have a baby of my own, a real life baby doll to have and to hold. Like a mirage, having a baby seemed like the most "fun" job, filled with puppy dogs and rainbows. And it is! Please don't hear me wrong. Being a mom is an amazing role, and I wouldn't have it any other way. But being a mother presents challenges that I had never anticipated.

Before entering motherhood, when I watched moms interact with their babies, all I could see was the tip of the iceberg. I didn't see the part of the iceberg underneath the water that was a lot more than I had expected. The lack of sleep, dirty diapers, diaper explosions, carsick toddlers, little ones needing my presence every minute of every day. Being a mom is a lot! You wear many different hats and become a jack of all trades.

Before I became a mom, I had this mirage idea of what being a mom would be like. My idea resembled a Stepford Wife holding a baby. This baby of course was not a real, crying, gasy, hungry baby. The baby I had composed in my mind was more like a baby doll, only it was living and breathing. The baby I imagined was a baby doll in all regards except for having joyful facial expressions, beautiful soft skin and hair, and a contagious laugh. Yes, being a mom would be like having a real life baby doll.

I was wrong. Being a mom is messy, and not always fun. Some days present major hurdles that leave me catching my breath by the end of the day. Being a mom sometimes requires that I sit out of certain events, social outings, and vacations that I would have otherwise taken. Being a mom demands sacrifice. It urges selflessness. Being a mom is a sanctification process.

I never knew how selfish I was until I had children. My little world revolved around me. My husband was in the picture, no doubt, but I was the forerunner. My job, my career, my books, writing, social media, getting my hair and nails done, my life revolved around me. Now, my life revolves around my kids, but even moreso, it revolves around Jesus. This sudden transition into mommyhood pulled the thick plush rug out from under me and landed me on my knees, crying out to Jesus for help.

The truth is, only the Lord can get you through motherhood. The Lord can be your strength when you let him. The Lord can be your daily portion. The Lord can fill you with more when your cup runs empty. The Lord can sustain your energy when your kids demand macaroni and cheese, and all you want is to be alone and have a few minutes to breathe.

The Lord can change your perspective of motherhood from burdensome to holy work. I now view motherhood as something that is holy and sacred. Motherhood was never meant to satisfy, fill, or bring us happiness. It was meant to draw us closer to our Heavenly Father. The meaning of motherhood is something so much greater than changing dirty diapers, grocery store trips, laundry, and dishes. Motherhood is a purification process in which the Lord rids us of ourselves, and reminds us of who we belong to. We are daughters of the King. Motherhood enables us to see, and realize that the driving force behind what it means to be a mother is Jesus.

Motherhood is a sanctification process that has deflated my blown up view of myself and has brought me back down to earth, back down upon my Cheerios ridden floor, on my knees seeking Jesus. Motherhood reminds me daily that this life is not about myself. Its purpose is Matthew 28:19, for us to "Go and make disciples . . . " The meaning of motherhood is that we become less, and Christ becomes more. Jesus is greater than our frustrations as moms. Jesus is greater than our worries for our children. Jesus is greater than the daily challenges motherhood presents.

> *We went through fire and water,*
> *but you brought us to a place of abundance. Psalm 66:12*

What if motherhood is a test? What if it is meant to refine us through the fire? After all, fire is the most efficient sterilization tactic.

Motherhood presents trials and tribulations similar to other seasons of life, but what sets motherhood apart is that these trials and tribulations sometimes involve our children. The tribulations motherhood presents stretch beyond just ourselves. These are the most difficult types of trials; those outside of our ability to control, those that pose threats against our children.

Similar to the Isralelites being led to the Promised Land, through the wilderness, the Lord will lead us and refine us along the way, throughout the course of being a mom. Family trials will refine our faith and make us cling to the cross of Christ for consolation and practical solutions. Like never before, motherhood will make us trust in and depend on Jesus' ability to heal, comfort, lead, and protect not only us, but also our children.

We will have desert and wilderness seasons of life. There will be struggles and we will face confrontation as mothers. In drawing closer to Christ through difficult chapters, we will grow in our faith, establish character, and enhance our ability to endure life challenges with a sense of perseverance welling up inside of us. Because we have the Well, the source of Living Water to draw from, we are equipped to face life's wilderness seasons with confidence, assurance, rejuvenation, and hydration, all found in Jesus, through God's Word and prayer.

## In Christ Alone

Being a mom does not define you. If you determine that your identity is found in the name, "mommy," then you are setting yourself up for future disappointment. The truth is that your babies will grow up and leave home, sooner than you know. It's going to pass by faster than you think. They say, "the days go slow, but the years pass fast." We only get 18 years with our children at home. The days add up, so we must make each one count! We must maintain focus on the cross throughout the course of motherhood, not only so that we can lead our children to Jesus, but also so that we can establish a firmly rooted foundation on Christ. We must continue to focus on the growth of the little mustard seeds inside of our own hearts, so that we will grow up to reach the full stature of all that God has for us as his followers.

> He told them another parable: "The kingdom of heaven is like a mustard seed, which a man took and planted in his field. Though it is the smallest of all seeds, yet when it grows, it is the largest of garden plants and becomes a tree, so that the birds come and perch in its branches." Matthew 13:31-32

Our identities cannot be found in being moms, because motherhood is just a season. And while yes, being a mom is for a lifetime, our kids are going to need us less and less, and unless we have Christ as our rock, the wind and rains threaten to damage or destroy our homes. Our hearts are meant to be cultivated and kindled in Christ's love and life giving presence throughout the course of our entire lives. Now and forevermore, our identities must be rooted in Christ alone.

> *Dear Jesus,*
>
> *We love you God. We pray that you would be our strength on days that seem like more than we can handle. We pray for your presence in our hearts and daily lives. We pray for your wisdom to fill us. We pray for your love to edify our deepest desires. Help us to remember to put you first, and to place our identities in you alone Jesus. Before being a mom, wife, or any other role, we place our full hope, trust, hearts, and lives in your hands. In Jesus' sacred name we pray, amen.*

## Steps of Faith:

- What was your perspective of motherhood before actually becoming a mom? Did you have a similar mirage experience? I know that being a mother can be tough, but what are some of the unforeseen blessings you have experienced? Consider the personal relationships you have established with each one of your children.

# Chapter 13

# "Quiet" Time

I was hiding out in my closet, desperate to have a few minutes to myself in God's Word. My parents were in town, playing with the kids, so I thought it was the perfect time for me to sneak away. My little girl, Emma Claire, toddled along after me, entering my closet just as I had cracked open my Bible. My initial reaction was disappointment, but we ended up reading Psalm 5 together, and it turned out to be a such a sweet time.

> *Listen to my words, Lord,*
> *consider my lament.*
> *Hear my cry for help,*
> *my King and my God,*
> *for to you I pray.*
> *In the morning, Lord, you hear my voice;*
> *in the morning I lay my requests before you*
> *and wait expectantly.*
> *For you are not a God who is pleased with wickedness;*
> *with you, evil people are not welcome.*
> *The arrogant cannot stand*
> *in your presence.*

*You hate all who do wrong;*
*you destroy those who tell lies.*
*The bloodthirsty and deceitful*
*you, Lord, detest.*
*But I, by your great love,*
*can come into your house;*
*in reverence I bow down*
*toward your holy temple.*
*Lead me, Lord, in your righteousness*
*because of my enemies—*
*make your way straight before me.*
*Not a word from their mouth can be trusted;*
*their heart is filled with malice.*
*Their throat is an open grave;*
*with their tongues they tell lies.*
*Declare them guilty, O God!*
*Let their intrigues be their downfall.*
*Banish them for their many sins,*
*for they have rebelled against you.*
*But let all who take refuge in you be glad;*
*let them ever sing for joy.*
*Spread your protection over them,*
*that those who love your name may rejoice in you.*
*Surely, Lord, you bless the righteous;*
*you surround them with your favor as with a shield.*
*Psalm 5*

After we read the Psalm, we prayed together and said "amen." I told Emma Claire, "Mommy loves God." She echoed my statement then added, "Emma loves God." It was such a special moment in time. I could not have asked for a better "quiet" time that day.

The truth is that our kids need to be getting to know God with and beside us, partaking in our quiet times. They need this godly example set before them so that they will follow after Christ's footsteps. I pray the Bible means as much to my daughter and son someday as it means to me and my heart.

*For you bless the godly, O LORD; you surround them with your shield of love. Psalm 5:12 (NLT)*

Psalm 5:12 is one of my all time favorite Bible verses. The Lord surrounds the godly with a shield of his great love for us. Some versions exchange the word "love" with the word "favor." Jesus surrounds us with his love and favor, each and every day, through every season.

Recently, my five year old nephew asked his parents to pray with him to accept Jesus into his heart. It was a monumental, joyous occasion for my entire family. My sister sent an encouraging text message to everyone shortly after the announcement of Paxton accepting Christ:

> I hope this message encourages you all (Tate and Ali) and all of us, as parents and future parents, to keep discipling Paxton and all of our kids to know the Gospel, and walk in the light by teaching them through the Word:
>
> *"But if our gospel is veiled, it is veiled to those who are perishing. In their case, the god of this age has blinded the minds of the unbelievers to keep them from seeing the light of the gospel of the glory of Christ who is the image of God." 2 Corinthians 4:3-4*
>
> The Bible commentary said that the "god of this age" is Satan. Though men love darkness and choose the darkness, Satan still works hard to keep them blinded from the light and salvation in Jesus.
>
> This commentary struck me a bit when it comes to children: Whenever men choose darkness it does not mean they are innocent victims of Satan's blinding work. But if children do not have good parental leadership then they will grow up to choose darkness every time.
>
> Praise the Lord that once our faith is in Jesus we cannot be blinded . . . distracted maybe but never fully blind to his goodness!

What truth! Once we are accepted into the family of God, we can no longer be fully unaware of the Lord's presence in our lives. We can be distracted and enticed by the temptation of sin at times, but never left alone in total darkness.

We must disciple our children and train them up in the ways of knowing and loving the Lord, so that they will have a candle to carry with them along life's way. Christ's holy presence is that candle. Our children need to know Jesus. They need to know Jesus personally and come to love him for themselves. They need Christ's Holy Spirit inside of them, guiding them along life's way. They need God's Word filling up their little souls. Each and every day they need to have the Bible read to them, and for their parents to pray with them. Because kids' minds are like absorbent sponges, they desperately need to hear God's Word and practice talking to Jesus, daily.

Encourage your kids to reach out and pray to Jesus. Pray with them, but also encourage them to talk to God on their own. While kids are very young, they can still be drawn to the light. 1 Thessalonians 5:19 says, "Do not quench the Spirit." Encourage your children to know Jesus for themselves, even at an early age. Involve them in your daily quiet times and do not quench the Spirit that is at work, moving in their little hearts.

Having quiet time to reflect on God's Word and pray to Jesus is so important. Even a few minutes a day can change your perspective, and draw you close to the heart of God. A daily quiet time will renew your heart and mind in Christ Jesus (Romans 12:2).

It is so wonderful to have isolated quiet times with the Lord, but as moms, this is not always a reality. Some days it is simply not in the cards for us to be able to sit down, by ourselves, and get in the Word. Many days, our children will be present. We can incorporate them in our quiet times on these days. We can talk to Jesus with our children when such seed sowing opportunities arise.

## Speak Up, Stand Out For Jesus

While daily quiet times are wonderful, there are moments in the lives of well known Bible characters who remained quiet at a time in their lives when it was crucial for them to speak up. Jesus' disciple, Peter disowned Jesus three times during the course of Christ's trial and crucifixion (Matthew 26). It was heartbreaking to Jesus. Although it was self-inflicted, it was heartbreaking to Peter as well. How many times do we deny Jesus in our daily lives, all the same, by making ungodly choices, conforming to the patterns of peer pressure in conversation, or by ignoring the call of the Holy Spirit for us to take action? I know I am guilty of such denials.

Sometimes the Holy Spirit calls us to walk outside the lines of our comfort zones in order for us to reach other people for Jesus. Whenever I started blogging about motherhood, and how being a mom relates to our faith, I felt very uncomfortable posting blogs on my Facebook account. While I felt uncomfortable, I also felt like sharing these posts was something the Lord had called me to do in order to encourage other moms in their daily walks with Christ. I stepped outside of my comfort zone and I have had positive feedback from other moms about how they have been encouraged by my writing. This being said, I have to admit that writing is not of or from myself, but all for the glory of God. It is all for Jesus. I pray everyday that he will give me the words to write. It is my job to walk in obedience and share what God has commanded me to.

In the same way, it is up to you to share your faith. In whatever way or shape this looks like for you, share. Share your testimony with others, share the Gospel of Jesus with your children, share words of encouragement with your husband, and speak the name of Jesus. Give God the glory in your everyday affairs. Insert Jesus' name and verbally acknowledge Christ in conversation whenever an opportunity arises. Follow the Lord's hand in your life. Listen to the Holy Spirit. Allow God to do his holy work in and through you. Do not remain silent on account of Christ, for you have been called and were created for such a time as this, to share Jesus with others.

*For if you remain silent at this time, relief and deliverance for the Jews will arise from another place, but you and your father's family will perish. And who knows but that you have come to your royal position for such a time as this?" Esther 4:14*

Queen Esther was faced with a major decision in her life, to speak up and risk her life on account of saving the Jews, or to remain silent in safety. Esther was encouraged by her uncle, Mordecai, to boldly approach the King's throne with a position of humble confidence. In this same way, we have the Holy Spirit inside of us, that urges us to do what is right. The Holy Spirit speaks to us and tugs on our hearts with a request for us to obey. Esther entered the King's court at a time when she could have been killed for such an interruption. However, the King extended his royal scepter and she was excused and invited to share her request. Because of Esther's bravery, the Jews were spared and the enemy, Haaman, the King's wicked advisor who instigated the plot to annihilate the Jews, was executed.

*The thief comes only to steal and kill and destroy; I have come that they may have life, and have it to the full. John 10:10*

There is a real enemy out there, lurking in the shadows, attempting to silence us on account of Christ. We must learn to listen to the Holy Spirit inside of us to know when to speak up and act, in order for lives to be saved for Jesus. The thief comes to kill and destroy people's lives and steal their eternity. Christ has come to give us abundant, eternal life in Heaven. Through knowing Jesus, receiving Christ's grace, and living lives of faith, we will be with Jesus someday. We are invited to accept Christ's invitations for us to share a word of his with others. He has called us to be bold. He has summoned us to walk with humble confidence, leading others to the cross. Let us be reminded that there is a time for quiet, but also there are certainly moments in time when we are put on the spot and must choose to boldly speak the name of Jesus.

*Dear Jesus,*

*Thank you for time spent in your Word. Thank you for daily quiet times, and for the ability to share your Word with our children. I pray that we would be diligent and faithful in this regard. Help us to equip our children through the Bible and prayer. Help us to love our children well, and lead them to you and your cross, each day.*

*We love you Jesus. Thank you for saving us, for paving a way, through your blood and scars. Thank you Jesus for your ultimate sacrifice. Help us to live boldly for you, unashamed of proclaiming your name. It's in the precious, perfect name of Jesus we pray, amen.*

## Steps of Faith:

- Have a quiet time with the Lord today. Whether it is during naptime, or with your kids, make it happen! Get in God's Word and pray.

Chapter 14

# Molding Hearts

*All Scripture is God-breathed and is useful for teaching,*
*rebuking, correcting and training in righteousness, so that*
*the servant of God may be thoroughly equipped for every*
*good work. 2 Timothy 3:16-17*

When my daughter and I play with Play Doh together, she insists that I compose intricate creations such as a bunny rabbit, Pooh Bear, and our dog, "Molly." Usually my clay figures do not turn out as exact replicas but resemble more Elementary versions of these same creatures.

When we attempt to mold our children's hearts to be more like Christ, we are not expert sculptures. Praise Jesus that there is grace in this regard! But, if we do not know Christ and have his Word and image written upon our hearts for ourselves then we will not be able to mold our children's hearts to be like that of Jesus. We must be seeking, striving after, and living for the Lord in order for our hearts to know his image, and for us to be able to sculpt our children's hearts into Christ's very own likeness.

*You were taught, with regard to your former way of life, to*
*put off your old self, which is being corrupted by its deceit-*
*ful desires; to be made new in the attitude of your minds;*

*and to put on the new self, created to be like God in true*
*righteousness and holiness. Ephesians 4:22-24*

We are called to a standard of holiness, and while there is grace in this regard, we should be working towards renewing our attitudes and minds to reflect that of Jesus Christ. Holiness cannot be attained through our own will power or by simply striving. We must be in our Bibles, getting to know Jesus. God's Word comes alive and awakens our hearts when we read it. We must read God's Word with the intent to learn from the nature of Christ's righteousness. We glean godly wisdom from experiencing the various facets of the holiness of God, through his Word.

It trickles down from the top. If we are not being edified daily, chances are that our children's hearts are thirsty as well. If the wellspring of Christ's character is alive and flowing inside of us, then we have Living Water to draw from and are better able to grace and rejuvenate our children's hearts. Like a mountain stream, we need the words of Jesus flowing down into the pools of our souls that overflow and carry runoff into our children's lives.

## Pray For Your Children

I have heard it said, "The chances are, if you are not praying for your children, then no one else is." While this strikes a minor, melancholy chord within me, it promotes an awareness to this potential tragedy as well. We need to be on our hands and knees, each day, praying for our children. *What types of things can I pray for in my children's lives?* I am so glad you asked!

Things to Pray Over Your Children:

- Pray that they come to know and love Christ
  for themselves someday.
- Pray for their health.

- Pray for good teachers, and other godly influences in their lives.

- Pray for protection over their hearts.

- Pray for their purity.

- Pray for their future spouses.

- Pray for guidance and favor in their future professions.

- Pray for the Lord's leadership in their hearts and lives.

- Pray that they would grow up to be spiritual leaders who influence others for Jesus.

- Pray that the Lord would protect them, guide, and watch over them all the days of their lives.

When Jesus was teaching his disciples how to pray, he prayed the following prayer, known as "The Lord's Prayer." We can use this same prayer that Jesus taught his disciples to pray thousands of years ago to pray over our children today.

*"This, then, is how you should pray:*

*"'Our Father in heaven,*
*hallowed be your name,*
*your kingdom come,*
*your will be done,*
*on earth as it is in heaven.*
*Give us today our daily bread.*
*And forgive us our debts,*
*as we also have forgiven our debtors.*
*And lead us not into temptation,*
*but deliver us from the evil one.*
*Matthew 6:9-13*

*Dear Jesus,*

*Precious is your name,*

*I pray that your Kingdom would be further established through the lives and the eternal impact my children are going to make for you someday.*

*I pray that your will be done in their hearts and lives, and that your Word be firmly rooted and established in their minds.*

*I pray that you give my children the mindset of Heaven and write eternity upon their hearts.*

*Give my children a word from you today Lord.*

*Forgive my children when they mess up and sin. Help my children to forgive those who sin against them. (Help me to forgive those who sin against them as well God.)*

*Please, please, please Lord Jesus, steer my children away from rocky treacherous paths that are not a part of your plan. Deliver them through your guidance and divine leadership in their lives. Amen*

Your prayers do not always have to sound this eloquent, but I think it would surprise you how easy it actually is to talk to God. Speak to him out loud. In your car, on your knees, at home, folding the laundry, speaking to the Lord is a daily discipline that will guard your heart and mind in Christ Jesus (Philippians 4:6-7).

Talk to Jesus about your children. Pour out your heart for your children through prayer. Chances are, you love your children more than anyone else does in this entire world. What better way to love your children than to pray over their hearts and lives each day?

*The Prayer Map For Moms* is a great resource, available on Amazon, that can help you pray for your children through journaling. It is only $7.99 for a hardback spiral bound copy and would be a great investment to make towards praying for your children. I super enjoy it because I like writing, but also because you can reflect back on previous prayers written and witness the way God has answered prayers in your children's lives. It is a powerful tool that has helped keep me accountable in praying for my children.

## Let It Shine! Let It Shine! Let It Shine!

I sell antiques online. It is my business and hobby, a part time gig, my "Mama Side Hustle." I really enjoy it! I get to buy antique and vintage items at local stores and go to vintage and antique shows both local and across the country to obtain quality inventory. The key is buying items that check off all the boxes of my buying criteria "hit-list" which goes as follows:

- Quality

- Desirability

- Condition

- Authenticity

- Aesthetics (Visual Appeal)

- Rarity

- Do I like it personally?

This buying criteria list was given to me by my precious mother in law who taught me everything I know when it comes to "antiquing." Her advice also includes the opinion that, "a low price is the worst reason to buy." I couldn't agree more! There are so many cheap objects out there that lack quality, authenticity, and appeal that may be discounted antiques, but still the worst reason to buy. The final item on the checklist, "Do I like it personally?" is an Alex addition to the list. I figure, if I really like the item, then someone else will too! (Fingers crossed.)

When it comes to our relationships with Christ, we must weigh our hearts and our daily motivations against this list as well. Quality, desirability, condition, and authenticity; we can skip the final few from the antiques hit-list, but let us zoom in on these four traits in regard to our hearts.

- Quality—Are we getting enough quality time spent in God's Word each day?

- Desirability—Are our thoughts desirable to God?

- Condition—What are the conditions of our hearts? Are all chambers open for Christ to have access?

- Authenticity—Are we being open and honest with God about our heartfelt needs and desires through prayer?

These are all important attributes when it comes to our relationship and walk with Jesus. We must be authentic with God and speak with him each day. We must cultivate our hearts and thought life to be at a standard of desirability to the Lord. The conditions of our hearts must be pure. The quality of our time spent in God's Word and on our knees in prayer is a determinant factor when it comes to the state of our hearts and connection to Jesus.

It all trickles from the top! We must have a God fearing, life breathing, loving, forgiving, generous, humble, and kind heart-attitude. If we want our children to learn from us and adopt the Christ ordained disciplines of godly people, then we are going to have to exude those attributes for ourselves. In order to mold hearts into Christ's likeness, we need to first check our own hearts in the mirror. Are there any blemishes? Are there any areas that we need to work on? Are there any chambers that we have closed off from the Lord that need reopening? Quality, desirability, condition, and authenticity are not just antiquing criteria. These attributes are good heart qualities that we need to acquire and adopt for ourselves. We must put on the nature of Christ, and become clothed in his very own righteousness.

> Therefore, as God's chosen people, holy and dearly loved, clothe yourselves with compassion, kindness, humility, gentleness and patience. Bear with each other and forgive one another if any of you has a grievance against someone. Forgive as the Lord forgave you. And over all these virtues put on love, which binds them all together in perfect unity.
> Colossians 3:12-15

In order to mold our babies' hearts and minds to resemble the pattern and likeness of Christ, we must cultivate and water the gardens of our own hearts before we attempt to water theirs. God will provide us with the wisdom and grace that we need to disciple our kids each day. Our job is to be in our Bibles and pray.

*Look to the Lord and his strength;*
*seek his face always. 1 Chronicles 16:11*

When I was little, my art teacher used to make a model of whatever painting or sculpture we were about to create. Our job is to do our best in forming our own hearts first so our children have a good model to go by. Still, the only perfect model is Christ himself, and that is why we need the presence of Jesus so very desperately in our lives each day.

We need to be running and chasing after Jesus in order to catch a glimpse of his glory. We need to reflect his image and light through the radiance of our hearts. Like a holy mirror, as Christians we have Christ's presence dwelling in us; therefore, we have the divine ability to reflect Christ's likeness. We will mess up and sin at times, but God is full of grace. We need to let Jesus shine through us by the way we live our lives. It's like the song, "This Little Light of Mine." We need to allow Christ's glory to reflect and shine through our hearts and daily lives in order for our children to get a better view of what Jesus is really like. His love, his compassion, his kindness, his humility, his gentleness, and his patience- these are the facets of Jesus that we need to refract light through. The world needs the hope of Jesus. Let Christ's light shine for your children and the world to see. *This little light of mine, I'm gonna let it shine . . .*

*He has shown you, O mortal, what is good.*
*And what does the Lord require of you?*
*To act justly and to love mercy*
*and to walk humbly with your God. Micah 6:8*

Let us walk humbly with God each day. I am going to be the first to admit that I am not perfect in this regard. I get pompous, blown up ideas of myself and this is not of or from God.

When the Egyptian slave masters, who oppressed the Israelites, were in command, they stood upon platforms as a means to intimidate and be able to look down upon their slaves. My friends, this is not what we are called to do or be as parents. As godly influences in our children's lives, we are to walk humbly before the Lord each day. This requires us to get down off of our platforms and get down on our children's level in order to reach them for Jesus.

So often moms threaten and intimidate their kids in hopes that they will not fall out of line. But what happens when they do? Do you approach them whip in hand (metaphorically speaking), or do you approach them in love and get to the root of the problem? With God's Word fresh on your heart, and the presence of Jesus alive and active in you, I pray that you would approach them gently, rationally, and out of love. It is my prayer that you would address and correct the problem in a similar way that Jesus did when he encountered sinners. Like those bracelets that were oh so popular back in the day, think, *W.W.J.D.* (*What would Jesus do?*) *How would Jesus address my child's sin?* Even in the moments when it would be so much easier to overlook the offense, we must be diligent and stay attuned to our children's heart-attitudes and corresponding actions each day.

In order to mold our children's hearts to be like that of Christ, we need to be actively working with and among them, not basking on platforms of glory. We cannot be isolated from their heart issues, or from their daily lives. We need to be in on the action! Let's make it happen.

Dig into those Play Doh containers, and pull out those peculiar miniature tools and animal-shaped cookie cutters. Get involved in your children's lives, and get busy applying spiritual tools in their daily lives. Scripture, prayer, and God's Word; these are the tools that will help form our children into men and women who love and live for Jesus. This is the goal. Our model is Christ. We must strive to be like him ourselves, because our children look up to us as a model when they are little kids, teenagers, adults, and beyond. We must teach them that as parents, we are imperfect and desperately need and depend upon Jesus. He is the perfect image we must look to and pattern our hearts after. We must teach our children to look to Jesus above all else.

*Dear Jesus,*

*Please pattern and mold our hearts into your image. Help us to influence our children for you Jesus. Show us ways that we can better sculpt their hearts to reflect your own. Jesus, we look to you to help us teach our children your holy precepts. Fill us with your Word and presence, each day. In Jesus' precious name we pray, amen.*

Steps of Faith:

- Purchase a children's Bible that resonates with your soul. Read it to your children daily. Watch and wait as the Lord speaks to your heart, in addition to your children's, by observing and meditating on God's Word through the lens of a child.

Chapter 15

# Loved

D o you ever have moments of doubt? I am not talking about the kind of fluffy doubt that you can easily brush off, I am talking about the type of doubt that creeps in, unannounced, like a flood in the night; the kind of doubt that destroys homes, hearts, and lives. I have been there.

One afternoon during naptime, I was on my knees crying out to God. I felt completely empty inside. That's when I could hear the Lord's prompting, a quiet whisper inside of my soul, *Trust Me.* Jeremiah 29:11 came to mind, followed by Proverbs 3:5. *For I know the plans I have for you Alexandra, plans to prosper and not to harm you. These plans are to give you hope for a bright future . . . Trust in me, and lean not on your own understanding. Acknowledge me in every aspect of your life, and I will make your path straight.* Sometimes when I pray scriptures like these pop into my mind and interrupt my anxious thoughts. The truth is, we are loved as moms; right where we are at, in the midst of our everyday, ordinary lives. God is able to find us in these seemingly mundane moments in time and transform us into his likeness if we allow God to do his holy work inside of us. We must open up our hearts and allow Christ's seeds in us to take root. We must let them grow and become firmly planted fruit bearing trees, able to provide food and shelter to others.

God wants to use us as mothers. Although some days feel ordinary and appear to lack true purpose, there is a deeper meaning no doubt. The meaning of motherhood is for us to become more like Jesus, and to grace our children's lives with the knowledge and understanding of God's love.

As mothers, I think we all struggle a little bit with feelings of inadequacy, like our lives don't always matter. I am here to tell you, you're wrong. You do matter. Your life matters, for Christ's Kingdom purposes. You matter so much to the heart of God. He created you on purpose, for his purposes. Your life is rich in meaning, according to Christ's Word. His plans are to prosper you. His plans are not to harm you. His plans are to give you hope for the future. Jesus loves you infinitely. On days when you feel empty inside, remember this truth.

> *The Lord appeared to us in the past, saying:*
> *"I have loved you with an everlasting love;*
> *I have drawn you with unfailing kindness. Jeremiah 31:3*

Think back to the first time you held your newborn child. Remember what it was like when the nurse handed you your brand new baby, placed her on your chest, and gave you a few minutes alone, to be in awe, wonder, and adoration of this precious new life. I'm sure it was a sacred moment in time for you, like it was for me. We love our children from the moment we lay eyes on them. In this same way, God loves us. He loves us even more than we love our children, and this is hard to fathom.

> *See what great love the Father has lavished on us, that we*
> *should be called children of God! And that is what we are!*
> *The reason the world does not know us is that it did not*
> *know him. 1 John 3:1*

When people are awestruck by our hope and joy found in Jesus, this should come as no surprise to us, because these same people who do not know Jesus do not experience hope in Christ.

We have a reason to be joyful, and on days that feel like the rain just keeps pouring down, let us be thankful for this reason alone. We have the hope of Heaven, the joy of Jesus in our hearts.

## Number One In Our Hearts And Lives

God loves us and considers us his children. We are children of God, heirs of the throne. As moms, teachers, doctors, lawyers, accountants, principals, and nurses, we are children of the Lord Most High. Before we place our identity in our professions, or in being moms, we must remember that our true identity must be found in Christ alone. It is so important not to lose sight, because all of these other things that we try to fill up our hearts with will leave us feeling empty inside if Christ is not the bedrock foundation of our lives.

Jesus loves us and wants to be number one in our hearts. He hears our innermost thoughts and knows when we prioritize other things before him. This is called idolatry. It is a sin, and it breaks the heart of God. Still it is so easy to do. We must fight against this unholy nature and seek to place Jesus on the throne of our lives, above all else.

Where do you spend most of your time, talent, and treasure? Check your bank statement. This will give you some major clues as to what is vying for your time and attention. How are you using your talents, and passions that God has given you to serve the Lord? Are you investing in the Kingdom or only in things of this world? These are some good questions to consider when it comes to confronting idolatry in our lives.

*But seek first his kingdom and his righteousness, and all these things will be given to you as well. Matthew 6:33*

The Bible gives us this promise, that if we seek first Christ's kingdom and holiness above all else, then our hearts will be full. "All these things will be given to you as well." I am not positive what "all these things" are, but I believe that when we seek Christ first and strive to live according to his righteousness then our hearts' desires will be satisfied. God has this divine ability to transform and alter what it is that we long for in order to make it align with the holy plans he has for us. "All these things" are surely God's goodness and blessings yet to unravel in our lives. When we place knowing and loving Jesus above all else, everything else will fall in line, according to God's perfect plan.

## Held

You are held. The Holy Spirit surrounds you with His love, grace, and protection. Jesus carries you when life brings you to your knees and disables you from walking on your own. We are like infants in the sense that we need to hold Jesus' hand. We cannot walk and stand on our own two feet because sin will creep up and knock us down, every time. We need Christ's strength. We need the Lord's fortification over our lives. We need Jesus' protection. We need his saving grace. We need the Holy Spirit surrounding us on all sides of our lives.

Jesus loves you Mama! Let him be the backbone of love and support in your daily life. Lean in on his Word, and cry out to Jesus on days when you feel weak. Jesus' power works best in weakness (2 Corinthians 12:9). Allow Christ's strength to gracefully fall on you. Welcome his love into your life with arms wide open. Place your full identity in Christ, and acknowledge him throughout the day. In all your ways, submit to Jesus who will love, protect, and care for you with the mighty love of a Heavenly Father.

*Dear Mama,*

*You are so loved. You are loved by the world and the people around you. You are adored by your children. Your husband loves you beyond what he is able to fully describe. Jesus loves you infinitely; every piece and part of you, even the broken pieces. Jesus is able to take what is broken inside of you and design something that is holy and beautiful, pleasing to the Lord. He loves you this much to transform what was broken by sin and remake it into something lovely and brand new. Jesus forgives you. We must ask for his grace, but when we do he gives it in full. The Lord withholds no good thing from those he loves who walk according to his will (Psalm 84:11).*

Although the world around you may seem to be in shambles, God is still present and working in your life. You have his holy light to guide you through the darkness. Praise the Lord for the gift of his Holy Spirit! Praise Jesus for his great love.

Don't forget, our God is mighty to save. Although the Lord might not pluck you from the darkness that envelops you at times, he will provide you with strength, sustenance through his Word, and the candle of the Holy Spirit. Jesus will never leave or forsake you (Deuteronomy 31:6). He loves you too much to let you get swallowed by the night. He loves you too much to allow you to drown by the tidal waves of life. He loves you too much to let go of your hand in the busy parking lot of this world.

Hold tight to your Heavenly Father, and rely on Jesus' great love to see you through. Jesus adores you. Never forget, you are wonderfully, fearfully, and beautifully made. You are infinitely, fully, and perfectly loved by the Creator himself.

*With Love,*
*Alexandra*

*For you created my inmost being;*
*you knit me together in my mother's womb.*
*I praise you because I am fearfully and wonderfully made;*
*your works are wonderful,*
*I know that full well.*
*Psalm 139:13-14*

Dear Jesus,

We adore you. Thank you for your love and daily grace in our lives. God, you are a good good Father. Thank you for your divine leadership, protection, love and comfort through our times of need. We praise you for your ultimate goodness evident throughout the course of our lives.

*We pray that your love would fill us more each day and that we in turn would fill our children's hearts with your great love. Thank you for giving meaning and purpose to our lives through the blood of Christ. In Jesus' mighty name we pray, amen.*

## Steps of Faith:

- Say these words with me: "I am loved. I am adored by my children, husband, and the Lord himself. I am fearfully and wonderfully made. Praise Jesus for creating me in his image, and making me a mom."

Chapter 16

# Ain't No Popsicle

O bedience is a daunting word. It carries weight. It is not one of those nouns that is fun and playful, like the word "popsicle" for example. Now that's a fun word! I love handing out popsicles. It's like being a living, breathing ice cream truck. Everyone's happy when the ice cream truck comes rolling through the neighborhood. Obedience ain't no popsicle! Obedience is not always fun and I believe it is meant to present a serious tone, because of the seriousness of its connotation. In light of what the Lord commands, we are called and required to walk in daily obedience to his divine Word and Will. We are to put God first in our lives, our family second, and our own wants and needs third.

I fail at this from time to time and will be the first in line to confess my failure when it comes to consistent, constant, and concise obedience. Sometimes I like to weave my own path and this leaves the loom in a giant, tangled mess. Christ has the ability to come in and untangle the rat's nests that I create from time to time, when I ask for his forgiveness. But I must walk in the light of Christ's redemption and obedience after the Lord helps me to start anew.

When we are obedient to the Lord, even when it seems like what we are called to is a giant task, a far fetched hope, a mile away dream, the Lord shows up and takes what we have to offer and multiplies our strength and resources. When we are obedient to the Lord, we set an example for our children of godly submission. When we are obedient to the Lord, we open up doors for our children to walk through, in the name of Jesus.

## Giants

Considering Biblical obedience, David was most likely 16-19 years old when he faced the Philistine giant, Goliath. Talk about a "childlike faith!" David went up against a giant who all of the other Israelite men cowered away from, a giant who is speculated to have been somewhere between 7 and 11 feet tall.

> David said to Saul, "Let no one lose heart on account of this Philistine; your servant will go and fight him."

> Saul replied, "You are not able to go out against this Philistine and fight him; you are only a young man, and he has been a warrior from his youth." 1 Samuel 17:32-33

David was a light of hope in his day and age, an emblem of promise to the Israelites who were thoroughly discouraged by Goliath. Still, before David's victorious defeat, Saul doubted David's abilities and capabilities as a young person. David was young, and small in stature in comparison to the physical traits of Goliath, but the Lord God was on David's side. He was the one who called David away from his sheep and fortified his heart with the courage to face the giant. He was the one who equipped David with a sling and five smooth stones. He was the one who gave David the words to say in response to King Saul's doubts, "The Lord who rescued me from the paw of the lion and the paw of the bear will rescue me from the hand of this Philistine." (1 Samuel 17:37)

In the same way that the Lord delivered David from beasts of the field in the past, David knew that God would deliver him from this giant as well. We too have faced beasts of the field in our pasts that should give us courage to press on and face the giants of our present and future. Based on God's history of faithfulness in our lives, we can be equipped as prayer warriors who walk in obedience to God's Word and Will. Even when God calls us to step out and be brave on account of his name, let us be obedient. Let us lean in on the prior knowledge and history of the Lord's faithfulness in our lives in order to walk boldly and confront the giants who will be present in our futures. Because we love and depend on God, let us face those giants with a sense of bold confidence because Jesus fights on our behalf. He goes before us and conquers our enemies.

We are called to be faithful and obedient to his callings as mothers and Christ followers. When the Lord puts something on your heart, don't ignore it for it is your divine mission to pursue the callings Jesus has for you. He has unique, intricate, custom designed plans for you to carry out for His Kingdom purposes. When God plants a dream or calling inside of you, do not ignore the Holy Spirit tugging on your heart! Say yes to God, and he will equip and empower you.

Be bold. Be brave. Be uniquely who Christ created you to be Mama! God has amazing dreams and plans for you. These plans are earth shaking, eternity making, soul changing plans that God wants to fulfill through you. Say yes to God's divine missions in motherhood and in life. Your children will be edified and inspired by your obedience.

Your children are spectators in this battle that we call life. You are training them up to be warriors of the King, by example. Fight for Christ. Your children will stand behind you in awe and wonder of the mighty God you serve and obey.

The Lord will fight for you. He will equip you with the stones that you need, and the sling required to propel those stones. He will empower you with bold confidence. He will amplify the force of the stones you propel in order to knock out whatever giant it is you are facing today. You need only to be obedient.

## Down the Rabbit Hole

Although the word, "obedience," presents a serious tone, it is actually life bringing when we follow the Lord's commands. When I was asked to be the Co-Leader of my women's Bible study, I was not sure if I was equipped. Still, I felt led through prayer that this was the Lord's will for me. I said "yes," to God and it has taken me deeper in my relationship with Jesus. It has fortified my daily dependence on the Word, and has caused me to enter into this whole other level of newfound awe and wonder in reading and discovering God's Truths found throughout the Bible. I have truly ventured "down the rabbit hole," in reading God's Word. In such a good way, "down the rabbit hole," I have gone, and I never wish to return from this wonderland. I have uncovered newfound Truths and am in daily awe and wonder of the goodness, holiness, and great love of our mighty God.

> He has made everything beautiful in its time. He has also
> set eternity in the human heart; yet no one can fathom what
> God has done from beginning to end. Ecclesiastes 3:11

Oceanographer Jacques Coustea once said, in regards to the spell of the sea, "it holds one in its net of wonder forever." Sadly, Coustea was not thought to have been a believer. If only he could have known and loved Jesus, maybe his love for the ocean would have transferred over to a love of God and his Word. The Bible truly does, "hold one in its net of wonder forever." The Bible is an eternal book. The Lord writes eternity upon our hearts as believers. Still, so many other distractions take over our daily actions and prevent us from getting into God's Word. What is it in your life that you need to forfeit and transfer over your time and energy away from in order to focus more fully on getting into The Word?

For me, it was my to-do list. It was too long, too demanding, too overwhelming. But once I chose to get into God's Word first and foremost, my perspective changed. I realize now that the "to-dos" in my daily life will always be present, and that I must fight to get into God's Word, first. We must place getting into God's Word above all else, because Christ is what this life is all about.

We hear God's heart through His Word. The Lord has something special to whisper to each one of us. We must listen to the Lord through his good, perfect, and pleasing Word. This is the Lord's Will (Romans 12:2).

> *The word of the Lord came to Jonah son of Amittai: "Go to the great city of Nineveh and preach against it, because its wickedness has come up before me."*
>
> *But Jonah ran away from the Lord and headed for Tarshish. He went down to Joppa, where he found a ship bound for that port. After paying the fare, he went aboard and sailed for Tarshish to flee from the Lord. Jonah 1:1-3*

The prophet, Jonah was initially disobedient to the Lord's request for him to travel to Nineveh and declare the Lord's grievances against this sinful place. It was too daunting of a task. The Ninevites were brutal, and sinfully vicious. Jonah feared traveling to Nineveh and declaring a message from the Lord God Almighty. He feared man, before fearing God and jumped on a boat, headed in the opposite direction, to Tarshish.

How often do we do this in our daily lives? We hear from God, but write it off as too grand of a task. I know I am guilty. Still, the Lord finds a way. I don't know about you, but I sure want to be used by God. The Lord will find a way to carry out his plans regardless of our own. Jonah was in the belly of a whale for three days before his decision to be obedient to the Lord's Will was sealed. God is capable of choosing someone else for his missions if we are uncooperative. Luckily, there was grace for Jonah and there is grace for us as well. Let us walk in obedience to the plans the Lord has for us. Approach God in prayer. Ask him what he has specifically planned for you.

*Dear Jesus,*

*We are grateful for your guiding hand in our lives. We trust you alone Jesus and fully rely on your Word, each day. We need more of you. Help us to be diligent in reading our Bibles and in prayer. I pray that you would reveal to us the task you have uniquely created, designed, and ordained for us to carry out, individually. Speak to our hearts and tell us of your plans. I want to be used by you, Jesus. Use me in accordance with your plans, according to your Word and your divine will. Show me what it is I am meant to do to glorify you, today. Strengthen me to walk in obedience. Speak to my heart Jesus. Amen*

## Steps of Faith:

- In what way do you feel the Lord commanding you to surrender over everything to live in complete obedience to God's Word and will? Is it generosity, daily diligence, or control? In what way is God calling you to step out of the boat, into the wind and waves, to walk on water, in complete obedience to Jesus?

Chapter 17

# God's Grace

*And if by grace, then it cannot be based on works; if it*
*were, grace would no longer be grace. Romans 11:6*

Grace is a heavenly word. It is used approximately 162 times in
the Hebrew version of the Bible. In light of God's Word, its
meaning is, "The unmerited favor of the Lord manifested through
Salvation."

We love the idea of grace. We believe in God's grace. We give
grace to our children. We act in accordance with God's grace. We
grace the world with acts of love and kindness. But, how often do we
share a little taste of this heavenly piece of pie with ourselves?

I don't know about you, but I am extremely hard on myself. I
give grace to others daily, but oftentimes fail to give myself a single
drop. Each day, I dig, and dig, and dig some more. I love and I
serve my children with all of my might. Still, I deny myself the
right to drink from the waters of God's grace and keep on digging.
This is not healthy! We must allow ourselves to drink from the
water bottle of God's holy grace, each day.

As mothers, we have a lot on our plates. Housework chores,
running kids to dance and soccer practice, getting lunches ready
for school . . . there are many many tasks that wearing the Mama
hat requires. Whenever I get a few spare moments to breathe,

I often get into God's Word. This is one way that I give myself grace. It's like drinking from a heavenly water bottle. In getting into God's Word I am rejuvenated, and better able to give myself and others God's grace freely.

Grace is kind, and wants the best for our lives. Are we being kind to ourselves and forgiving of our faults? I tend to hold grudges against myself. I replay old broken records of my past; times when I messed up, experienced mom fails, and sinned. God has given us his grace in full and when he forgives, he forgives us one hundred percent. We are to step forward in the light of God's grace, each new day.

With grace, confidence, and assurance from the Lord God, we are to conduct our lives in a manner that exudes the fact that we are chosen, forgiven, and set free. We are forgiven from our past sins and mistakes, and set free from the condemnation of our every single former mom failure. Through forgiveness, because of what Christ did for us on the cross, we receive God's grace in full. As mothers, as wives, as daughters of Christ, we have been chosen and are called to live accordingly; to dance in the light of God's redeeming grace.

> *Praise be to the God and Father of our Lord Jesus Christ,*
> *the Father of compassion and the God of all comfort, who*
> *comforts us in all our troubles, so that we can comfort*
> *those in any trouble with the comfort we ourselves receive*
> *from God. 2 Corinthians 1:3-4*

Praise be to God for Christ's compassion, comfort, and grace. May we shower it upon others. May we allow its life-giving drops to rain down upon ourselves.

The world's standard for moms nowadays is virtual perfection. Facebook, Instagram, and Snapchat have exuded motherhood in a light that has impossible standards. Posting newborn pictures of your child, every month, for the first twelve months; having extravagant birthday parties every single year; creating picture perfect Christmas cards; these are only a few of the fallacies. There are many, many more mommy mandates. No, these are not requirements; but yes, there is real pressure to live up to these society imposed expectations when it comes to being a mom. While these things are not bad things, if they are taking away from our personal walks with the Lord, distracting us from Jesus, then that my friend presents a serious threat. We need to have grace for ourselves when it comes to the world's standards of motherhood, so that we can fight the good fight of faith, and put Christ first and foremost in our lives.

Which race are you running? Are you running the Mom of the Year Sprint, or are you running the marathon of a life full of faith, hope, and love that God has called us to? We need to be careful that we are choosing our race wisely. It all stems from how we spend our time. Social media poses some serious threats against moms in this day and age. While social media is not bad, binge scrolling on Facebook and Instagram is not what I would describe as edifying. It is draining. People's social media selves are controversial to their real life personas. This is what we do not see when scrolling. Social media does not present to us real life and our minds play tricks on us and insist that it is the real deal, and what we ourselves should strive for. Be careful how much time and mind energy you attribute to social media. We must make choices each day to do things with our time that fill up our hearts.

> For the grace of God has appeared that offers salvation to all people. It teaches us to say "No" to ungodliness and worldly passions, and to live self-controlled, upright and godly lives in this present age. Titus 2:11-12

Because of God's grace, we are called to a higher standard. We are called to a heavenly standard and must live life with eternal life in mind. We must set our thoughts on the sight of Heaven, and store up for ourselves treasure that will last and matter in eternity.

> "Do not store up for yourselves treasures on earth, where moths and vermin destroy, and where thieves break in and steal. But store up for yourselves treasures in heaven, where moths and vermin do not destroy, and where thieves do not break in and steal. For where your treasure is, there your heart will be also. Matthew 6:19-21

Motherhood is laced with God's grace. We are going to fail as moms. There are times when we are going to forget to pack the dessert in our child's lunchbox, arrive late and are last in the pick up line, and are not going to remember . . . sorry I forgot what we weren't going to remember. There will be times when we are not going to remember, period! The motherhood brain fog syndrome is real. We must fight against our tendencies to forget special little things that matter big time to the hearts of our children. But, there is God's grace present and available to us each and every day. We will experience mom fails at times throughout the course of motherhood, but we must brush ourselves off and get back up again, in the light of God's grace, in the name of Jesus.

*Dear Jesus,*

*Thank you for your love and grace. You are mighty to save and quick to forgive. We praise you for your goodness, Lord. Please forgive me of my sins, the times I mess up and fall short of your glory as a mother. Forgive me, and set me free from condemnation. Allow me to walk in the light of your mercy, grace, and freedom in full. In Jesus' perfect name, amen.*

## Steps of Faith:

- In what way can you acknowledge God's grace in your life? Take a bubble bath, get a Starbucks coffee, or go get your nails done and thank God for his grace and undeserved love in your life.

Chapter 18

# Joy in the Journey

There is a microstory found in *The Many Adventures of Winnie the Pooh*, (my daughter's favorite book and movie), where Rabbit conjures up a divisive plan to lose Tigger. Rabbit is so fed up with Tigger bouncing through his vegetable patch that he attempts to "take the bounces right out of him," through this unkind plan. Rabbit, Pooh, Piglet, and Tigger set off on an expedition early the next day and attempt to lose Tigger in the fog and mist. Their plan backfires. Instead of losing Tigger, they get lost themselves. The next day, when they are discovered, Rabbit says to Tigger, "You're supposed to be lost." Tigger responds enthusiastically, "Tiggers never get lost!"

Sometimes in life, we are going to get a little lost. Although we are supposed to be the ones who have it all together as moms, sometimes we will get lost in the fog. The trick is knowing the way home, regardless of the mist life brings. Like Tigger, we must decipher our surroundings and be able to get back on track and rediscover the path God has for us when we go astray.

Life will attempt to lose us in the heavy fog of our shortcomings and sinful nature. Through God's Word and prayer, we have a map. The Holy Spirit is our compass guide. Let us look up to where our help comes from on days that appear misty, when we feel lost and alone. Let us seek Jesus through life's harsh weather conditions and fortify our faith in the Lord. We will get lost, the trick is knowing who to look to in order to be found.

The compass arrow of our hearts and lives must point to Jesus. Through the thick and thin seasons of motherhood, let us seek to reflect God's glory. Let us be like compass arrows to our children that point up and away from ourselves, and to Jesus. When life gets dark, confusing, and seemingly hopeless let us be examples as mothers who cognizantly use the compass of God's Word and Jesus' presence through prayer, to find the way home.

*But he knows the way that I take;*
*when he has tested me, I will come forth as gold.*
*My feet have closely followed his steps;*
*I have kept to his way without turning aside.*
*I have not departed from the commands of his lips;*
*I have treasured the words of his mouth more than*
*my daily bread. Job 23:10-12*

I love this cluster of verses from the Bible, the words of Job. To put these verses into a broader lens of context, Job was declaring his innocence in response to his friend Eliphaz's confrontational attacks. His friends were convinced that Job had sinned and was being punished through a series of unfortunate tribulations, which was not the case. Job was being tested, through the fire, to prove his innocence and pure loyalty to the Lord God.

It is the prayer of my heart that these words spoken by Job, reflect my life. We steer where we stare, and so we must focus on Christ, fixing the eyes of our hearts on the cross. We must have God's sense of direction for our lives in mind. This godly sense of direction can be attained by becoming immersed in God's Word.

In order to come out "as pure as gold," we must go through God's refining process. The high temperatures, trials, and tribulations are seemingly unbearable at times. Motherhood is not for the faint of heart. It is a purification process. Sometimes the Lord refines us through the fire. But, this painful procedure is not without purpose. God's plans are *for* us, always.

In order to reach the state of pure and perfect gold, we must endure the fire and remain strong in the Lord, in the strength of his might (Ephesians 6:10). We must trudge through the trenches of motherhood at times, in the process of becoming the woman God has created each one of us to be. God created you special. He created you strong. He created you perfectly for the task of raising up your little men and women for Jesus.

We must rely on God's Word more than our daily bread. More than our phones or coffee cups, the Bible is our source of edification. When everything else is empty inside of us, we must seek Jesus. God's Word can replenish our every need.

The getting there process of motherhood can be a long, slow wait at times, while other days are a roller coaster of thrill, excitement, and emotion. "Are we there yet?" We continue to ask the Lord. While our question is desperate and rushed, God's response is slow and steady. "You are exactly where you need to be, at this precise moment in time."

> *Wait for the Lord;*
> *be strong and take heart*
> *and wait for the Lord.*
> *Psalm 27:14*

Hang in there mommy! We are not there yet, but there is hope in the waiting, in the process of becoming all that God created us to be as moms. There will be love, laughter, and tears throughout the ups and downs of motherhood; but ultimately there is joy in the journey.

> *But those who hope in the Lord*
> *will renew their strength.*
> *They will soar on wings like eagles;*
> *they will run and not grow weary,*
> *they will walk and not be faint.*
> *Isaiah 40:31*

## Sands of Time

"Every day is better than the last!" The biker man shouted in my direction. I believe he was trying to encourage me. You see, I was struggling, trying to carry my 36 pound toddler to the car while pushing a stroller. We had just left the Children's Museum and everyone was wiped out, mommy included. I love what the man said to me. Not only did it put a smile on my face, but also it stopped my mind in its tracks long enough for me to consider the reality that we as moms face. Motherhood is like an hourglass. The sands of time just keep slipping through our fingers and we can never get them back. Our children will continue to learn and to grow. In this way, "each day is better than the last." We must be intentional with our time and heart energy while our children are under our roofs.

Sand keeps accumulating at the bottom of the hourglass of this thing called motherhood and life. The sand will never return to the top. In this same way, we only have a certain amount of time, a set number of days with our children in our homes. We must strive to make every moment count with our kids, to be present in their daily lives, and to immerse them with God's love while they are under our roofs and reliant on our care.

Our children will continue to grow and become. They will grow into adults and will continue to become the people God created them to be. We must water our little seeds, faithfully. Our children have been entrusted to us. We are to disciple our children, and hope and pray that they will grow up to disciple others in this same heart changing way.

> "Again, it will be like a man going on a journey, who called his servants and entrusted his wealth to them. To one he gave five bags of gold, to another two bags, and to another one bag, each according to his ability. Then he went on his journey. The man who had received five bags of gold went at once and put his money to work and gained five bags more. So also, the one with two bags of gold gained two more. But the man who had received one bag went off, dug a hole in the ground and hid his master's money.

*"After a long time the master of those servants returned and settled accounts with them. The man who had received five bags of gold brought the other five. 'Master,' he said, 'you entrusted me with five bags of gold. See, I have gained five more.'*

*"His master replied, 'Well done, good and faithful servant! You have been faithful with a few things; I will put you in charge of many things. Come and share your master's happiness!'*

*"The man with two bags of gold also came. 'Master,' he said, 'you entrusted me with two bags of gold; see, I have gained two more.'*

*"His master replied, 'Well done, good and faithful servant! You have been faithful with a few things; I will put you in charge of many things. Come and share your master's happiness!'*

*"Then the man who had received one bag of gold came. 'Master,' he said, 'I knew that you are a hard man, harvesting where you have not sown and gathering where you have not scattered seed. So I was afraid and went out and hid your gold in the ground. See, here is what belongs to you.'*

*"His master replied, 'You wicked, lazy servant!* Matthew 25:14-26

God has entrusted us with children. Maybe you have seven children, maybe four, three, two, or just one. Regardless of the number, the Lord has blessed and entrusted you with children to raise. They are like the bags of gold in this parable.

Jesus wants us to affect our children's hearts and further his Kingdom. We play such an integral role. We must share Jesus with our children. Even when it feels unnatural, a little uncomfortable, or inconvenient, we are to share Jesus with our children, each and every day. I do this by reading a children's Bible to my kids and praying with them. It is appropriate for their young age. Once they get a little bit older, I intend to read God's Word, and give them a blank notebook to draw a picture about what they hear and learn. Someday, they can also write about what they learn. These are just some ideas of mine that I hope will help give you a starting point.

Begin getting into God's Word with your children today! Someday, I want the Lord Almighty to be able to say, "Well done my good and faithful servant." I want my bags of gold to be multiplied. The Lord has entrusted us with Salvation. We are meant to share it with our children. Do not hide it in your heart. Let your light shine bright for Christ as a mom.

> *"You are the light of the world. A town built on a hill cannot be hidden. Neither do people light a lamp and put it under a bowl. Instead they put it on its stand, and it gives light to everyone in the house. In the same way, let your light shine before others, that they may see your good deeds and glorify your Father in heaven." Matthew 5:14-16*

In all things, we are to glorify God. This starts in our homes. Glorify your Father in Heaven who sent his only son to die for you. Blatantly, verbally, repetitively share the love of God, the life of Jesus, the Gospel message with your children. In this way, we bring honor to all that the Lord has entrusted to us through eternal life.


## I Hope You Dance

One day, I was watching my little girl, Emma Claire, at her ballet lesson. It was one of her very first lessons, and she was just standing there, staring at the teacher who was dramatically doing the motions, flailing her arms, and trying desperately to get these two and three year olds to follow her dance moves. Some of the little girls were dancing. Emma Claire, however, just stood there in awe and wonder. She was taking it all in. While it was sweet and innocent for a little while, my prayer is that Emma Claire will learn how to dance on her own. I hope that she will learn to follow the teacher's dance moves with her own two arms and legs, and move to the beat of the music.

As Christ followers, we are called to dance. We are not meant to remain baby Christians who simply stare. We are not meant to be spectators who simply onlook. We were created to be belles of the ball. We were destined to dance for the King.

I hope you dance mama! I hope you live for Jesus and love with all that is in you. I pray that you would use your own two hands and feet for the glory of God. I pray that you learn to listen to the beat of the Holy Spirit's callings in your life, and act accordingly. In the words of Lee Ann Womack, "I hope you dance."

Dancing each day for Jesus is a choice. It is up to us to let our hearts skip in tune with the plans and purposes the Lord has for us as mothers and wives. I know some days are challenging, but we can do all things through Christ who strengthens us (Philippians 4:13).

> *I know what it is to be in need, and I know what it is to have plenty. I have learned the secret of being content in any and every situation, whether well fed or hungry, whether living in plenty or in want. I can do all this through him who gives me strength. Philippians 4:12-13*

These are the words of Paul, written to the church of Philippi. Paul was in prison when he wrote these words to the church. He was in chains, but his heart for the Lord could never be captured or tied down. He continued to preach the name of Jesus, despite his persecution. We are going to be persecuted as moms who follow the Lord. Not physically, but spiritually and emotionally, the enemy is going to attack and attempt to put us in chains. Never stop dancing for Jesus. Despite what this world tells you, Jesus is the Way, the Truth, and the Life (John 14:6). Stick to your mama guns when Satan tries to tell you otherwise through his lies.

The enemy is going to try to do anything and everything to knock you down, to put you in chains, to prevent your heart from spilling over into your mouth on account of Christ. He is going to try to shut you up. *Speak anyways.* When it comes to confrontation, I know some moments are uncomfortable but we are called to rise up in this modern day and age as Mamas who speak the name of Jesus.

The joy is in the journey . . . getting there can be so much fun! But this joyful journey is also laced with tears. Being a mom presents some challenges that are heart wrenching, terrifying, and full of sorrow.

> *Be joyful in hope, patient in affliction, faithful in prayer.*
> Romans 12:12

I cannot guarantee you consistent happiness as a mom, but Christ guarantees us his presence, peace, and joy in full. God wants to carry you through your trials, to hold your hand when life gets tough. The torque of this world wants to twist us away from Jesus, but we need to cling tight like never before. We need to apply the wrench of God's Word to work on our hearts each day, to turn our screws in the opposite direction of the ways of the world. The G-Force winds of life are going to come and try to knock us down. We need the bedrock foundation of our houses to be built upon the solid Rock of Jesus Christ. All other ground is sinking sand. Our phones, social media, even our husbands; these externals cannot be the foundation of our lives. Only Jesus will be able to fill our hearts. Jesus can provide for us in a way that nothing else can.

> *The thief comes only to steal and kill and destroy; I have come that they may have life, and have it to the full.* John 10:10

Only Jesus.

## Steps of Faith:

- In what way can you point the compass arrow of your heart and life in the direction of Jesus? Is it by mentioning, and giving God glory in conversation? Is it through choosing joy despite your circumstances? Is it by blessing and serving your spouse? Point the arrow up and away from yourself, toward Jesus today.

Chapter 19

# Mama Hearts

CONTRIBUTIONS BY SHERIDAN SALMON,
KELLY MOSS, AND LINDSAY MORRIS

I asked a few friends of mine who are rockstar mamas if they would be willing to share their thoughts and perspectives on motherhood. Their vantage points and experiences are all a little different, but come together beautifully to illustrate the meaning of motherhood through the lens of the Gospel.

## My Story

### By Sheridan Salmon

From an early age, I dreamed of being a mom and planned to stay home with my children. I was so thrilled to welcome my firstborn son in 2015, four months before my thirtieth birthday. I loved him so much, yet my transition to motherhood, and specifically life as a stay-at-home mom, was more gut-wrenching than I anticipated.

I wasn't mentally ready to lose so much sleep. I slept nearly every night for almost thirty years, and my body and mind were shocked by the sleep interruptions that came with life as a new mom. My first baby was a decent sleeper compared to most babies. However, for his first nine months he wasn't sleeping the same eight hours I wanted to sleep! I felt so exhausted! Sleep deprivation hit me hard and seemed like it would never end.

My new title—"stay-at-home-mom"—also threw me for a loop. The struggle itself was disorienting because I expected to stay home after I became a mom. So why am I not loving it? What is wrong with me? I didn't even like the term "stay-at-home-mom." Moms don't actually stay home all the time, do they? I definitely liked getting out! Day to day life with a baby is weird. You are needed 24/7 with random down time.

For the first time in my adult life, I didn't have a title or a pay-check. I struggled with people's perceptions of me. Before becoming a mom, people seemed impressed by my jobs. I felt that once someone learned I was a stay-at-home-mom, they lost interest. In reality, some people did tell me how wonderful it was that I stayed home with my son. I was the one who devalued what I was doing and failed to see the importance of my presence in my son's life.

During this time, I didn't know many stay-at-home moms, which contributed to my sense of isolation. Only one friend in our small group at church also stayed home with her child, so I felt like most of the people in my community didn't understand my life. We didn't have family in town or extra money for baby-sitters, so I didn't have consistent help.

Our family also went through a major transition around this time. Shortly after our son was born, my husband Caleb decided to open his own law firm (on a credit card—with no savings!). Dave Ramsey would have been horrified. We began Financial Peace University shortly before Caleb decided to take the plunge. Other couples in our FPU group were paying off debt and we got into more debt!

I do have to give Caleb credit; after losing my income we weren't going to make enough where he currently worked. Thank-fully, he had the vision for what he could build and has higher risk tolerance than I do! All this did not make it easy though.

For months our finances were extremely tight. I had a limited weekly grocery budget and went to Aldi once per week. One of our vehicles stopped working so I lost my freedom to get out of the house. I didn't have extra money to decorate our home or go to lunch with a friend. It was just me and my baby who couldn't talk.

This was definitely a season of change in my life and our family. It was exposing my faulty foundations of identity (title, pay check, others' opinions) and joy (hello Hobby Lobby and beautiful home!) While meaningful work and creating a lovely space are good things, God was using motherhood and our financial situation to prune me. I truly believe while it was a hard season, the fruit that came out of it (and is yet to come) is more than worth it. But it still took me time to surrender to motherhood.

## "Surrender to Motherhood"

Over the years I wrestled with finding significance and purpose as a mom. All my struggles with identity, title, importance, not earning a paycheck, people's perceptions of me (real or imagined)—were all deeper heart issues from which the Lord wanted to deliver me. Motherhood was the catalyst. Early in my journey as a mom, I continued to hear the Holy Spirit whisper "surrender to motherhood."

I did not surrender right away! Sometime after my son's first birthday, I thought the solution to my restlessness was to work part-time. I decided to start a wedding planning business. I worked hard, built a website, advertised, and organized a styled photoshoot. While I learned things through the experience and had some fun, I hadn't made any money after over one year and decided it was time to close. Although I felt God's permission to pursue it at the time, I finally realized it wasn't going to succeed as a business concept. The call to "surrender to motherhood" grew louder.

Complete surrender to motherhood felt like a death. By setting aside my pursuit of anything beyond my life as a wife, mother, homemaker, and friend I felt I was giving up control. Pursuing other interests felt like "doing" something.

There's a message in our culture that if we're not "following our dreams" then we're somehow missing out. But what if we're looking at it all wrong? What if motherhood is the pathway for God to usher us into our future calling? Motherhood has the potential to shape a woman's character in ways nothing else will if she lets the Holy Spirit sanctify her through it.

Statistically, millennials stay at a job for less than three years. Motherhood builds patience and perseverance through the tough and seemingly boring times. I loved the freedom before motherhood when I could change jobs when I wanted or more easily pursue my interests. But I couldn't quit being a mom. I had to set aside my self-interest, and put my child before myself, and stick with something that sometimes felt hard.

In surrendering to motherhood I had to accept greatness in God's eyes instead of the world's. I might not have an awesome social media page or receive praise by others for accomplishments, and that is okay. I still matter and my life is significant apart from anything the world notices.

As time passed, I realized God could bring any dream or aspiration I had to fruition overnight by His grace. I didn't have to strive, push, or "hustle" (women love that cliché word for some reason!) Whatever God wanted to do through me, He could and would make it happen at the right time.

Our calling is to be faithful.

## A Rainbow Baby

Tragedy and crisis really has a way of shocking us to change our perspective and realign our priorities.

In December 2017 our second son Wesley was born at 40 weeks 3 days of pregnancy. Within hours of his birth we learned he had a serious congenital heart defect and would need surgery. Sadly, Wesley had complications following a procedure and passed away January 3, 2018. He was 10 days old. Of course, our hearts were broken.

Grieving the loss of your baby is so painful. I went through all the stages of grief. I had long talks with God. I struggled to be around other babies. Of course we loved and wanted Wesley but we also wanted more children and decided we didn't want to wait long before we had more.

On March 21, 2018, the first day of spring, I got a positive pregnancy test! The hope I felt in the middle of my grief was such a gift. I was expecting our rainbow baby.

Pregnancy after loss has its own challenges to overcome— fear, what if's, happiness about the baby you're carrying but grief for the one who died. Even though I was pregnant, I still struggled to be around other women with babies or images of "normal" hospital experiences, and pictures of big siblings meeting the baby. While those happy moments often seem routine, after a loss you are acutely aware of everything you and your family missed out on. You learn to take nothing for granted.

With my firstborn I stressed about the house being messy and sleep schedules. But after Wesley passed away I realized how little those things matter in the big picture. Who cares if the house is a mess? Who cares if the baby isn't sleeping well as long as he is healthy and home with me? I gained a perspective that cost me greatly, but it helped me be more present and grateful.

When I was pregnant with our rainbow baby, it didn't feel real that I was going to take the baby home. But it was important to me that I lived by faith and trusted God, so by the third trimester I decided to live like I'm bringing our baby home. I bought things for the baby and I decorated the nursery.

My oldest son had an anchor themed nursery. For our rainbow baby, I decided to do a mountain theme. A song that spoke to me during this time was "Climb Every Mountain" from The Sound of Music. I remember as a kid thinking how long and boring this scene in the movie was! But now I love it.

Losing my second son and expecting our rainbow baby helped me realize that motherhood is something I wanted and it is a worthy dream to pour my heart and life into. I can love my children everyday and shape men and women of God who will love God and love others.

This shift in thinking doesn't magically make motherhood perfect or end mundane tasks and frustration with my children. I still need a break and I occasionally have an existential crisis about my choice to be a stay-at-home-mom! But the gift of perspective does make these tough moments easier.

By the way—our rainbow baby Connor arrived in November 2018. He was perfect! He brought so much healing to our lives. "Thanks be to God for His indescribable gift!" 2 Cor. 9:15

## Motherhood, A Calling

### By Kelly Moss

"What do you want to be when you grow up?" I remember being asked this question from a young age, and I never really was clear on the answer. I remember drawing a picture of a zookeeper on one assignment in elementary school and telling someone else I wanted to be a meteorologist.

Turns out I'm not too keen on cleaning up animal droppings and am terrified of tornadoes. Any other Oklahoma girls out there? Despite my misgivings on my career path from childhood to adulthood, there was one thing I wanted to be that never changed. A mother.

I grew up in what most would call a traditional family, living with my mom, dad, and older sister. We were blessed that my mom could be a full-time stay-at-home parent for most of my childhood. I have so many memories of playing games by the fireplace with my mom, picnics at the park, her braiding my hair, and making up stories about an imaginary girl named Silly Sally. I loved those special times together and knew I wanted to be a mom someday and have my own children to laugh at my own made-up stories with.

I started working in a marketing job at a nonprofit right after I graduated from college and several years later met my sweet husband. He, too, wanted a family. A couple of years into our marriage, after two miscarriages, we welcomed our sweet baby girl, Ellie, into the world.

I was thirty when I gave birth to Ellie and had seen more than a few friends have their own babies and raise them into toddlerhood. "This is going to be easy," I thought. "If they can do it, I can do it. I am an unselfish, mild-mannered woman. The transition from singleness to marriage wasn't that hard. This won't be either. I've got this."

I quickly learned that what I had was a false perception of what motherhood would look like and of the areas God wanted to work on in my life. Was that me who said I was unselfish? Standing over a crib at 3 AM with my crying baby girl lying below, I was met with many conflicting emotions. "She needs me. I'm tired. I want to help her. I can't take this crying anymore."

Did I love my baby girl with my whole heart? I am as sure of this fact as I am sure that ice cream is the perfect end to almost any day. What left me unsure were the less-than-perfect emotions that I was experiencing as a new mom.

I remember one night that God met me there in one of those moments and presented me with a thought that has stuck with me and has given me peace and strength through my first few years of motherhood. It was as if I heard God saying, "What would my love for you as a father look like in this situation?"

He reminded me that I, often, am like that helpless baby in the crib. God doesn't wait until a time convenient for Him to provide me with comfort. He is there to provide loving comfort no matter my temperament. He is patient and kind no matter how many times I cry out for help.

As my daughter has grown into toddlerhood, it has been amazing to watch her grow, learn to walk and talk, and gain a sense of humor and fierce independence. I often say to my husband, "She didn't used to exist. This is so cool!" I can't even imagine God's thoughts as he looks down on us, not only as a parent, but as our Creator.

One night during Ellie's bath, I was sitting on the ledge with my feet in the tub. She grabbed my arm and pulled me down so my face was touching hers. She smiled, and when I pulled away, she grabbed my arm and pulled me close again. I happily pressed her cheek to mine.

I had been there the whole time watching over her playing in the water, but she seemed to forget and asked me to come closer.

I so often do the same with our Heavenly Father. He is always there watching over us, but I often forget going about my daily life. I often panic and ask God to pull close when I feel alone or scared, forgetting that he has always been there. I am so thankful that He, too, pulls me close, reminding me of his presence again and again.

When I look at my daughter, I wonder who she will be when she grows up. The possibilities seem endless, but no matter what path she chooses, I pray that she grows up to be a woman who knows God and seeks to be more like Him every day. What an honor to help guide her in that direction as a mother.

Back to my original question—What do I want to be when I grow up? I, too, want to be a woman who knows God and seeks to be more like him every day. While much of motherhood is about teaching our children, perhaps we forget the incredible ways God uses motherhood to teach us about Himself and grow us in character to become more like Him. I look at mothers and women I look up to and respect, and I know I am far from the woman and mother I want to be. The greatest surprises I have experienced in motherhood are a more profound understanding of God's love and how God uses motherhood daily to refine me and shape me into the woman and mother He has called me to be.

## A Beautiful Sacrifice

### By Lindsay Morris

Before I became a mom, I had visions of grandeur of what being a mom would look like. I am an enneagram 7, and therefore, life is one big party. If I could spend my days at parks traipsing through tulips, I would. In my mind, motherhood was going to be all about playing with my kids and having tons of fun!

Alas, motherhood has been *a lot more hard work* than I could have ever imagined. Sure, we have our fun adventures at the zoo or the park or on the slip n'slide in our backyard. But mostly, motherhood is work. As a working mother of two young boys, I have found this season to be the hardest, and at times, the most stressful of my life.

Yet, there is purpose in it. Not just for me, but also for my kids. God has a purpose for their lives even at these tender ages— even when they're so young that they may not remember these years.

When your kids are young, mothering can seem all-consuming. They need you almost nonstop. And in the rare moments you get to yourself, you desperately need sleep!

This season of sleep-deprivation and mothering young children goes by quickly, though. Just recently, my older son transitioned to a booster seat, and seeing him buckle his own seatbelt makes me teary-eyed, realizing he is growing up and gaining more responsibilities by the day.

In my relatively short time as a mother, here's what I've found to be the meaning of motherhood:

If we are Christ-followers, then our purpose in every relationship is to make disciples. So ultimately, *the meaning of motherhood is to create disciples.*

Yet, ultimately, we don't get to choose for our children if they become followers of Christ or not. You can't force someone into a genuine faith in Christ. You can't make any guarantees that just because you take your kids to church regularly, read the Bible with them and pray with them, that they will grow up and become Christ followers.

Even if you put them in Christian school their entire education, that doesn't guarantee that they will decide to follow Jesus as an adult. Even if you homeschool them yourself and teach them everything you know about God and the Bible, you can't choose for them how they will live their lives.

How many of us know adults who were raised in incredible Christian homes, but have strayed from the faith and are living far from the path that their parents hoped they would stay on? Recently, I did a study on the book of Proverbs through The Village Church (Flower Mound, Texas). My eyes were opened to the meaning behind the well-known verse, "Train up a child in the way he should go: and when he is old, he will not depart from it (Proverbs 22:6, KJV)."

I've always taken that verse literally. OK, I'll train up a child in the way he should go. I'll do my part. Then God promises that my child won't depart from the path, right?

Well, not quite.

While the Bible is full of promises, the book of Proverbs is full of principles; not promises. A principle is different from a promise. A promise is a guarantee that something will happen, but *a principle is not a guarantee*. It is a tenet providing a general framework. In general, most children who are trained up in the way they should go will not depart from that way. However, it's not a guarantee.

Does that mean we should throw in the towel and just say "que sera sera . . . whatever will be"? Of course not. Jesus' final commandment to His disciples in Matthew 28:19 was, "Therefore go and make disciples of all nations . . . "

Our purpose in life is to make disciples.

If we're meant to make disciples of all nations, that command certainly extends to the small "nation" of our own families. *Our greatest discipling should occur right in our own homes.*

With that in mind, *how do we raise up disciples?*

1. **Create an environment that is conducive to following Christ.**

   - Is Jesus the center of your home? Are you pursuing Him as a family through regularly reading the Bible, praying together and attending church? Or are you so busy that attending church and incorporating daily habits that help you grow in your faith are not priorities?

2. **Pray for your children.**

- Kids are encountering so many worldly influences. Pray for protection over their minds and bodies. Pray for the right influences to enter their lives (friends, teachers, coaches, etc.). In addition, it's never too early to start praying for their future spouse.

3. **Set an example.**

- If you're regularly an unhappy, grouchy, yelling person, ask yourself, "Is this the type of person my child would aspire to be?" If you're full of joy, loving and kind, they will want to follow Jesus and have the same kind of fruit in their lives that you produce.

I believe that our main purpose in motherhood is to raise disciples. Through this process of discipling, though, *we are changed ourselves.*

Godly motherhood transforms us into more Christ-like women.

You may have noticed an immediate shift as soon as your first child entered the picture. You went from having a sleep schedule of your own, to being awoken every 1-3 hours by a crying, hungry baby. Your time was no longer your own. If you were nursing, your body was no longer your own either. Motherhood is sacrifice.

Outside of the physical sacrifices, motherhood requires a sacrifice of our desires. It could be small desires, like not being able to go out for a girls' night with your friends because you're putting young children to bed. Or it could be big desires, like giving up your career for a season.

As a full-time working mother, at times, I have wrestled over whether I should be a stay-at-home mom or not. This decision is personal to each mother, and I greatly respect my friends who have made the decision and feel called to stay home and raise their children.

I cherish my time with my children, but I have felt called to stay in the workplace. Even though I have continued working (except for maternity leave) during my children's early years, that doesn't mean I haven't made sacrifices in my career. My career offers countless numbers of networking opportunities and after-hours meetings. I have made a decision that I will not attend an evening or weekend meeting unless it is mandatory.

A professional women's organization I serve on the board for holds most of their meetings on weeknights. I've simply let them know that weekend evenings are sacred for me and my family, and I will not be able to attend the meetings.

I haven't given up my career altogether, but with these choices to limit my time commitment to work, I have limited my career advancement. I am a goal-oriented, highly driven person, but for this season, I realize that I can't have it all.

"You can have it all, just not all at the same time," said writer Betty Friedan.

I'm OK with not climbing the corporate ladder right now. I'm OK with not pursuing my MBA right now. I'm OK with not getting a promotion at work.

Because I realize that with those career advancements would come more time commitment and more responsibilities outside my home.

Someday, I will be able to advance in my career again. But for right now, I am in a coasting pattern career-wise. *Motherhood is a sacrifice, but it's a sacrifice well worth making.*

Philippians 2:3-4 says, "Do nothing out of selfish ambition or vain conceit, but in humility consider others better than yourselves. Each of you should look not only to your own interests, but also to the interests of others."

*Motherhood forces us out of our own selfishness.* It forces us to look to the interests of others. As we meet the needs of these little human beings, if we allow Christ to shape us during this season, we will adopt life-long habits of selflessness and sacrifice that please Christ.

*Dear Jesus,*

*Please create in me a selfless heart. Mold me into a beautiful creation of the best mom that I can be. Even when the sacrifices required are difficult, Lord, I pray that I will choose what is right. Help me to make God honoring choices in motherhood. Thank you Jesus for making the ultimate sacrifice for my sins in dying on the cross. Thank you for giving me the hope of spending eternity with you someday in Heaven. In Jesus' precious name, amen.*

## Steps of Faith:

- Motherhood is a sacrifice. Prayerfully reflect on components of your life that you have sacrificed in order to be the best mom that you can be.

- Journal a response to the question, "What is the meaning of mothood in light of Christ?" Incorporate some of your own personal experiences. If you would like to share what you wrote with me, I would absolutely love to hear from you! Message me on Facebook at "The Meaning of Motherhood," (https://www.facebook.com/MeaningMotherhood).

Chapter 20

# Motherhood

M otherhood is like a box of chocolates, you never know what each new day will bring! You hope and pray for good health and happiness, but sometimes calamity strikes. You long for peace and joy, only to be interrupted by a baby screaming from his pack and play. You desire holiness, to be a good mother, and to honor the Lord, but occasionally are on your phone too much and in your Bible not enough. Mama, I have walked in your shoes. I know the kind of determination, endurance, and perseverance it takes to be a "good" mother, on a daily basis. Even so, the truth is that sometimes I fail. The reality is that we all fail at times. Our "mom fails" do not define us, because Christ came and died for us. Christ's love refines us. There is this amazing thing called grace that we need to give ourselves and other moms on a daily basis. Christ gives us his grace freely, each and every day. We simply need to ask.

> "So I say to you: Ask and it will be given to you; seek and you will find; knock and the door will be opened to you. For everyone who asks receives; the one who seeks finds; and to the one who knocks, the door will be opened.

*"Which of you fathers, if your son asks for a fish, will give him a snake instead? Or if he asks for an egg, will give him a scorpion? If you then, though you are evil, know how to give good gifts to your children, how much more will your Father in heaven give the Holy Spirit to those who ask him!" Luke 11:9-13*

More important than being a "good" mother is to be a godly one. Although unstated, it matters to the hearts of your children and husband. Most of all, it matters to the Lord God. So often we worry about our children, but are we worrying about our souls first and foremost? We must get into God's Word. We must devote time daily to prayer. We must get off of our phones, stop scrolling, and choose time spent with Jesus.

Let's be honest here! We all have sin and fall short of the glory of God (Romans 3:23). What should set us apart from other moms who do not know Jesus? It is plain and simple; love. We must love God. We must love others. These are the first and second "greatest commandments," according to Jesus (Matthew 22:36-40). Love God, and love people.

I know that having and raising children presents roadblocks and inhibits our abilities to always be able to volunteer, carry out groceries for the elderly woman, and do things that we otherwise could do if we didn't have our hands full. But, how are you encouraging other moms? How are you being a light to your children? How are you loving and serving your husband? These are departments that we can zoom in on throughout the course of motherhood. These are areas in which we can exude God's grace and love.

When I first set out to write this book, I thought it was kind of silly and questioned God. *Why me?* I wondered. I am just a relatively new mom without the kind of experience and exposure that other, more seasoned moms have acquired. The Lord does not choose those he qualifies, but rather, those he calls. In what ways do you hear the Lord calling you? He wants you to step out of your everyday mom comfort zone. He wants to use you for his Kingdom building purposes.

Jesus calls us out among the wind and the waves. We will sink if we try to walk on the water by our own strength and willpower. Only God is able to do the impossible. Our job is to be obedient when he calls and to have faith in Jesus. Do not ignore the gentle whispers of the Holy Spirit in your heart. Jesus has called and destined you for greatness, because you are a daughter of the King. It's time to get out of the boat Mama! Jesus is calling.

## Lead Them Well

I've heard it said that being a mom is like "having your heart walking outside of your chest." It is life-giving to watch your children grow up. It is exhilarating to watch them develop into little people. It is breathtaking to watch them advance in their physical milestones. It is mystifying to kiss your baby goodbye and watch them walk into school by themselves, for the first time. It is heartwarming to watch them develop a curiosity of Christ. We must water this curiosity and help it to grow. We must encourage our children in their spiritual journeys. We must love them with the love our Heavenly Father has for us, and lead them well.

The source of our children's knowledge of Christ stems from us, and therefore we must immerse our children's minds in all that Jesus entails. Through reading God's Word, prayer, singing songs about Jesus, and so many other little ways this is accomplished. As mothers in Christ it is up to us to make it happen. We must infuse our children's minds with God's great love for us. We must shower their hearts with the wisdom of The Word. We must teach our children right from wrong. We must correct and discipline our children when they go astray. We must strive to guide them by the light of the lamp of Christ's love and leadership exuded in our own lives.

The Lord is our Shepherd, we are his sheep. He has entrusted us with his baby sheep. He has blessed us with lambs of our own to nurse and to love with the love of Jesus Christ. He loved us so much that he walked this earth, experienced fear, emotions, temptation, and pain in full, so that he could perfectly relate to us and comfort us in our weaknesses. Let us comfort our children with Christ's compassion in their weaknesses as well. Let us lead them to the Shepherd when correction is called for. Let us lavish their lives with wisdom. Let us pour out our mama hearts in prayer over their lives.

There are so many different ways that we can pray for our children. We can pray for their spouses, for protection over their hearts, for godly leadership in their lives, and for them to receive Salvation at an early age. We must practice praying for our children, daily. Make it a habit. While there are many different ways to pray, above all else, we must pray that our children will come to know, love, and live for Jesus for themselves someday.

Make disciples wherever you go, but most of all make a dent in the hearts and lives of the little people God has graced and placed before you. Raise up your children in the knowledge, love, and Fear of the Lord. Make disciples of all nations, certainly; but first and foremost, make disciples of your children.

> *These commandments that I give you today are to be on your hearts. Impress them on your children. Talk about them when you sit at home and when you walk along the road, when you lie down and when you get up. Deuteronomy 6:6-7*

Motherhood is uncovered in the Bible through the lives of many godly mothers such as Mary, Hannah, Eve, Rachel, Sarah, and Jochebed to name a few. These mothers were brave. They were strong in the Lord, and trusted in God's plan for their lives. They raised their children up in the love and admonishment of the Lord, and we are called to do the same.

> *And we know that in all things God works for the good of those who love him, who have been called according to his purpose. Romans 8:28*

God's "yes" in our lives might look a little different than what we expect, or even hope for at times. Still, God's plans are *for* us, not against us. We can trust God with our futures, and with our children's futures, because we know that we serve a good, good Father.

*But the plans of the Lord stand firm forever,*
*the purposes of his heart through all generations.*
Psalm 33:11

Based on the history of God's faithfulness in our lives and in the Bible, we can trust God and rest assured in the hope of his plans. He holds us in the palm of his hand. He carries us through life's storms. Even though some moments in life might not feel good, are uncomfortable, or unfortunate, we can trust that God's very best "yes" for our lives is going to unfold, according to his strategic plan and perfect timing.

*"I have told you these things, so that in me you may have*
*peace. In this world you will have trouble. But take heart!*
*I have overcome the world." John 16:33*

Sometimes motherhood is just plain difficult. Jesus is greater than our daily struggles as moms. He is greater than the everyday challenges and tasks that being a mom demands. He is greater than the emptiness we feel at times. He is able to fill our cups, daily, with his divine strength, and provide his holy portion for our heart needs.

*I urge, then, first of all, that petitions, prayers, intercession*
*and thanksgiving be made for all people—for kings and*
*all those in authority, that we may live peaceful and quiet*
*lives in all godliness and holiness. 1 Timothy 2:1-2*

Having a daily quiet time with the Lord in God's Word and prayer is so important to our mama hearts. In order to be able to provide God's love and abundant joy to our children, we must seek the source of everlasting abundance for ourselves through quiet time spent with the Lord, each day. When our children find us hiding out in our closets with our Bibles, seeking Jesus, this is the perfect time to involve them in our daily quiet times. After all, daily quiet times do not have to be so quiet. We must strive to involve our children in God's Word, and install reading the Bible and prayer as a daily habit in their lives as well as our own.

*Therefore, if anyone is in Christ, the new creation has come: The old has gone, the new is here! 2 Corinthians 5:17*

Like playdoh, we must strive to mold our children's hearts into the image and likeness of Jesus Christ. There is grace for us in this regard. Jesus was the only perfect disciple maker. Even so, we must fervently and prayerfully try to infuse our children's hearts with the love and knowledge of the Lord, each day. We must conform our little one's minds to the pattern of Christ's holiness, or else the world threatens to impress its mold.

*. . . And I pray that you, being rooted and established in love, may have power, together with all the Lord's holy people, to grasp how wide and long and high and deep is the love of Christ, and to know this love that surpasses knowledge—that you may be filled to the measure of all the fullness of God. Ephesians 3:17-19*

As mothers and daughters of Christ, we are loved infinitely by the Creator Himself. Jesus died for us in order to demonstrate his great love, and to make a way for us to be with him in Heaven someday. Jesus' love for us is hard to fathom. We must live from the source of his great love. Before all else, we must write the name of Jesus on our hearts. He is the King of our lives. Nothing else can satisfy the desperate longing that each and every one of us face. Jesus is the secret ingredient to a life of joy, fulfillment, and purpose.

*God blesses those who patiently endure testing and temptation. Afterward they will receive the crown of life that God has promised to those who love him. James 1:12 (NLT)*

Obedience is not always pleasant or fun, but it is what the Lord has called us to. Obedience ain't no popsicle, but we will reap a heavenly reward if we are diligent to obey his Word and will for our lives. We can demonstrate our love and sold out devotion to the Lord through obedience.

*He has saved us and called us to a holy life—not because*
*of anything we have done but because of his own purpose*
*and grace. This grace was given us in Christ Jesus before*
*the beginning of time.* 2 Timothy 1:9

While we will experience "mom fails," mess up, and sin, God's grace meets us in the midst of our shortcomings. The Lord desires our obedience, but we all have sin. We all fall short of God's glorious standard (Romans 3:23). We are going to mess up again and again. Jesus' grace is an amazing, precious thing. When we seek the Lord's forgiveness, he gives us his grace in full. In turn, we are to accept his grace for the precious gift that it is, and walk in a new light of mercy and love, lavishing God's grace and compassion upon others. We are to live lives of freedom through Christ. Because we have been forgiven and are set free, we are to live fully and love abundantly, in Jesus' name.

*Love the Lord your God with all your heart and with all*
*your soul and with all your mind and with all your strength.'*
*The second is this: 'Love your neighbor as yourself.' There is*
*no commandment greater than these." Mark 12:30-31*

There is joy to be found in the journey of motherhood. Because of Christ's peace and presence in our daily lives, we can be joyful despite the difficulties we encounter. I hope you dance each day for Jesus, like it is your last. I hope you live a life that has been repurposed for Christ. I hope you love the Lord God with all of your heart, mind, and strength. I hope you love your children with the kind of tender love that Jesus has for us. I hope you lace God's grace, care, and compassion throughout every little interaction you have with your children.

## Compass Arrow

God wants to use you mama, right now, wherever you are at. In your home, at the park, at school, at the aquarium, at church, or even the grocery store, God wants to employ you for his Kingdom purposes. He has created you uniquely and has given you special gifts and abilities to be able to preach the Good News to your children and those around you. That is what motherhood is all about! Live out your purpose. Walk according to God's Word. Lavish your children with God's love. Carry out the Lord's Will for you as a mama. Be a compass arrow that points to Jesus. Live out Matthew 28:19, The Great Commission, "Go and make disciples of all nations . . . " Remember, the disciple making process starts in your home, but keep a watchful eye out for other mamas, and those around you who might be in need of Jesus' love.

Be sure you are filling up your own heart, each day. God wants us to come, sit at his feet and enjoy being in his presence, like little children. Let us adopt a childlike faith and lean in on Jesus' love and comfort for us, through his Word and prayer, every single day.

The Bible has some amazing things to say. Let us get into the Word and seek Jesus wholeheartedly. Let us read God's Word to learn more about the holy nature of the Almighty God we serve. Let us strive to learn about and become more like Jesus. His life, love, death, and resurrection become fresh in our hearts, and have the ability to change our daily perspectives when we seek him through his Word.

Take care of yourself Mama! I know that some days are tough and require us to call upon every last ounce of strength within us. Jesus wants to meet us in our weakest moments and fortify us with his love, energy, and care. Let God's Word be like the energizer bunny to your life. Call upon the Holy Spirit to fill you in moments of despair.

As mothers, Christ followers, and human beings, we all have one thing in common, our desperate need for Jesus. Before filling up your mind with the ways of the world, seek Jesus. Before reaching for your phone, scrolling through social media, or getting that second cup of joe, acknowledge Christ's presence in your life. Get into the Word. Deepen your relationship with our Lord and Savior, Jesus Christ.

God loves you so much and wants you to live a full life. His plans are for us! Even on days that lack sunshine, our God is divinely orchestrating a sweet symphony of the plans he has for us.

We have the hope of a bright future, because the Lord is in control. As a mom, I don't like the feeling of not being in control, but God has got us. Right where we are at, in our homes, he hears our hearts and answers our prayers according to his way and will, in his perfect timing. Trust in the plans God has for you.

Live a life of trust and take leaps of faith for Jesus. Puddle jumping is absolutely something we were meant to do. As Christ followers, jump from puddle to puddle. Don't worry about getting wet! God created the rain. In Jesus name, take leaps of faith in life, and daily strides towards holiness.

Motherhood is meant to refine and purify our lives. It rids us of ourselves and draws us closer to the heart of God. Allow motherhood to do its holy work inside of you. Open up your heart and the Bible each day. Get on your hands and knees and pray. Let the light and love of Christ shower its morning dew upon you, through every season, each new day.

Through the laughter, love, and tears, depend upon your faith in Christ, hope in God's plans, and the love of Jesus to carry you through motherhood. Jesus is calling you. Step out of the boat, into the wind and waves, and be brave. As a Christ follower, dare to be different from other moms. Be bold in your faith. Speak the name of Jesus.

Christ loves you as you are, flaws and all. His love and grace are received in full through Salvation and repentance. We will mess up as moms. We will fall short as wives. There are new morning mercies and grace for us, every single day.

> *Because of the Lord's great love we are not consumed,*
> *for his compassions never fail.*
> *They are new every morning;*
> *great is your faithfulness. Lamentations 3:22-23*

We will never be perfect on this side of Heaven, but we are on a journey of becoming a little more like Jesus, each day. With every nose wiped, each diaper changed, through every after school pick up line wait, by means of bodily fluid cleanup, doctors appointments, disappointing moments, and happy days; we are becoming more like Christ through motherhood. He has placed little people in our lives for us to feed, care for, play with, correct, love, and disciple each day. What a blessing it is to be a mom; a special gift; the Lord's provision for our lives. Motherhood is a divine mission. It is an opportunity to further the Kingdom of Heaven and allow Christ's holiness to cultivate in our lives.

For such a time as this, you have been called and created to be a mom for Jesus. You are doing God's holy work. Allow his holy work to change you. Soften your heart and allow Jesus to mold you into his perfect image.

Jesus loves you mama. Love him in return by dedicating your whole life to him. Give every piece and part of yourself to Jesus. Allow God to remake you to be "the kind of woman you'd want your daughter to be;" "the type of wife you'd like your son to marry someday."

Point the compass arrow of your life, up and away from yourself. Reposition the arrow of your heart to be fixed in the direction of Jesus, on a daily basis. This is the Meaning of Motherhood. Be an encouraging arrow, pointing other mothers, your children, husband, and all who know you to our Lord and Savior, Jesus Christ.

## Hope In The Struggle

*Cast your cares on the Lord*
*and he will sustain you;*
*he will never let*
*the righteous be shaken. Psalm 55:22*

I used to struggle. I struggled with being a mom and no longer having my identity secured as a classroom teacher. I struggled with developing new patterns and routines as a new mom. I struggled in being a stay at home mom initially, and felt extremely guilty because I knew I should have been nothing but grateful. And I was grateful, but it didn't make the struggle any less real. If anyone knows that being a mom is not only physically challenging, but also mentally it is me. I want you to know that there is hope. There is bright light at the end of the tunnel. Our babies don't stay little forever. They are not always going to need their diapers changed, or to be bottle fed. They will eventually be able to go potty all by themselves, and even wash their hands. I know it's hard to believe when you are in the midst of caring for your child's every need. But try to enjoy it. Try to savor the moment, because it will not last. Motherhood is always changing, our kids are always growing, and we must press on to continue to grow in our relationships with Christ along the way.

Jesus is our source of hope and light. On days that seem dim, lean in on the love that Jesus has for you. He loves you infinitely, every piece and broken part of you. Jesus wants to remake you into something that is a stained glass mosaic masterpiece of his glory. Motherhood may break you, but allow God to remake you into something even more beautiful than what you were before.

Being a mother may be the most beautiful thing we do with our lives, second to following Jesus. He is number one in our hearts and lives, forever and always. Praise Jesus for his eternal presence, for saving our souls. Praise Jesus for the sacred gift of motherhood.

*Dear Jesus,*

*I pray for your hand over us, as mothers, and as your daughters. I pray that you will bless and protect us. You know our every need. You are the Alpha and Omega, Beginning and the End. We need you, desperately, each day, every hour, every second. We need your guidance and divine wisdom spoken over and into us through your Word. We need your confidence and protection running through our veins. We need to trust in your kindness and lean in on your love and support through prayer and God's Word. We need accountability. We need to take action steps toward executing your divine plan for our lives. In the small and the great tasks alike, Lord we pray for obedience to your will. Lord, we pray that you would send people and put circumstances into our lives that would enable us, and spur us on to be more like you. Like a breath of fresh air to our lungs, God we need you. Help us to trust in, cling to, and rely on you more each day, Jesus. We need your guidance. We need your grace. We need your wisdom. We need your forgiveness when we fail. We need your propelling fire in our souls. Come alive in our hearts. Pour out your love, goodness, mercy, and life giving power over us. Help us to live chosen for you Jesus, to grace our children's lives, and to reach a hurting world that is in desperate need of you. In Jesus' wonderful, almighty, precious, and powerful name we pray, amen.*

*Her children arise and call her blessed;*
*her husband also, and he praises her:*
*"Many women do noble things,*
*but you surpass them all."*
*Charm is deceptive, and beauty is fleeting;*
*but a woman who fears the Lord is to be praised.*
*Proverbs 31:28-30*

## Steps of Faith:

- Focus on your inner beauty by memorizing scripture. Memorize Proverbs 31:28-30.